DREAMING WORLDS AWAKE

Books by the same author:

PATHWAY INTO SUNRISE; Journey of a Wounded Healer
                                                Horus Books

CLEA AND THE FIFTH DIMENSION
                                                StarDrum Books

THIS STRANGE AND PRECIOUS THING
                                                Horus Books

Also available at www.esmeellis.co.uk

DREAMING WORLDS AWAKE

STORIES, SYNCHRONICITIES, DREAMS AND
CORRESPONDENCE,
with a scatter of poems

New consciousness, New energy, New writing.
Crossing frontiers

HORUS BOOKS

2011

Publication copyright © 2011 Esmé Ellis

First published in Great Britain in 2011
by
Horus Books,
Bath, BA2 5DL, UK

Esmé Ellis has asserted her right under the Copyright, Designs and Patents Act, 1988, to be identified as the Author of this work.

All rights reserved. No part of this publication may be reproduced in any form or by any means without the prior written permission of the publisher.

ISBN 978-0-953392-82-7

esme.ellis@btinternet.com

Cover and inside illustrations by Esmé Ellis

Copy-editing, design and typesetting by *Tuff Talk Press*
robert_w_palmer@lineone.net

DEDICATION

For Artibella Agnes

*Dances in the rain,
dances with rainbows.*

"Your dreams at night are potent fields of
creativity, understanding and wisdom."
Adamus — Saint-Germain, January 2011

CONTENTS

An INTRODUCTION	7
1: DREAMS – INCLUDING CORRESPONDENCE	9
2: SYNCHRONICITY	19
View Over Atlantis	20
3: CYBERSPACE	26
4: STORIES About a Tortoise	29
Dido	34
More Dreams	35
Another Dream	37
5: DREAM INTO POEM Climbing with Dido	40
Incantation for Dido	42
9: ANOTHER STORY – AND MORE CORRESPONDENCE	44
Blackbird Singing	45
10: FRAGMENTS ON THE WIND – A SCATTER OF POEMS	49
11: ANOTHER JOHN: ANOTHER SHAMAN?	51
12: SYNCHRONICITY – TOPPING THE CHARTS	64
Adam	68
The Rock Drill	71
Jacob, the Angel and Me.	74
Heading into the New: The Dark Angel	77
Once More Synchronicity Intervenes (Crysse's Poem)	80
13: ZONE SHIFT	87
Universal Feedback	90
14: IN A NUTSHELL	99
Expect the Unexpected	106
15: TALE OF A FISH	114
16: LION STORY – Coda	116
17: THE JOURNEY I TOOK	121
ACKNOWLEDGEMENTS	123

AN INTRODUCTION

After spending four or five years on my last book, a work of fiction, I was beset by the urge to begin writing again. It gave me no peace. A 'follow on' story, a new novel, maybe a stab at science fiction; I made several starts, but it was all drivel. I had a plot; that was not the problem. I even engaged the interest of another author who agreed to be my 'writing buddy'. He recommended sci-fi books to read dealing with the same theme, a set-in-the-future, secret establishment creating laboratory designed babies for the rich and powerful. I researched, I began again – and again, but the story lines fizzled out. Where was I going wrong?

Around this time I'd met, via cyberspace, the Australian author, Marisa Calvi. She had also recently published a book, *Pharaoh Thutmose III, a channelled life-story of Kuthumi Lal Singh*, and I responded eagerly to an invitation to 'dialogue' with this Ascended Master, through her. I put my concerns about my creative block to him. *It's hardly surprising you can't seem to write this story,* he told me, *it's pulling back memories of the horrors which you and others were involved with in the time of Atlantis before its destruction. That's all in the past now. Let it go. Much better to write something new, but keep it light and fun.* Unsure to what extent the 'light and fun' would prevail, nevertheless, from the moment I took in his comments, my writing began to flow once more.

Something new, something different and unplanned. I would simply write whatever came, naturally and freely. I

INTRODUCTION

would allow that which was alive and creative in me to express itself. I would be open to new voices from both inside and outside myself. Of its own volition something began to take shape. Stories arose, dreams came, a poem or two, a letter here and there. And above all, amazing instances of synchronicity which confirmed my growing feeling that when we stand in the moment, in the Now, in trust and faith, then the Soul, the Universe, the Greater Self, call it what you will, stands ready to support and enter into a co-creative alliance with us. What I hadn't been prepared for was, that as I journeyed through one year of present time, presences from the past, notably that of the sculptor, Sir Jacob Epstein, would make themselves known to me. Nor had I anticipated that this dialogue with Kuthumi would expand to form the major part of the Correspondence.

DREAMS – INCLUDING CORRESPONDENCE

To begin at the beginning – yet there is no beginning: no beginning, no end; but a story has to have one – and so does a book, so I'll begin here :–

It was this dream, the example I'm about to relate, which sparked off the idea that dreams could be stories in their own right, full of drama, and if you look deeper, full of symbol, mystery and mythology. Dreams may not have a plot with logical consistency, (though they're capable of surprising us on the odd occasion even on that). They defy our mind's concept of time sequence, but, in my experience, they have an underlying construct which, while not always appearing to have an obvious meaning, may, if you learn to 'live alongside' them without pressing for instant disclosure, reveal their secrets later, *in their own good time.* Or if not– if the meaning still eludes us– then because we've honoured the dream by giving it space, paid it our attention, our Dreamer Self might offer us another, a sequel dream, or in some cases a 'second chance to view' which throws light on the one we missed earlier.

Of course if you favour the Freudian theory then dreams, along with the expression of art and religion, will be evidence of a neurotic personality or stem from delusion and infantile regression– and of course he was forming this theory upon examples which some very disturbed patients brought to him. For him they manifest the unconscious, and

DREAMS – Correspondence

I have no quarrel with that, but to suggest that The Unconscious is either a receptacle for trivia or material censored by our conscious mind is to deny ourselves access to a playground of boundless discovery and spiritual (i.e. consciousness) expansion. I believe his one-time colleague Carl Jung was nearer the mark – his theories far more promising. And this is why I'm happy to include a letter from John Moat which came in response to an account of a dream which I sent him.

I didn't meet John Moat until about a year after we began corresponding. John is a writer, artist and poet in his seventies. His artistic output ranges across a wide canvas; his sketches are quirky, his wit is warm, his humour hides profundity and his satire comes with lashings of hilarity. He has been doing the Didymus column in Resurgence for almost forty years and when the post brought me a copy of his newly published collection, *The Best of Didymus*, drawn from that magazine, I took it into the garden to read. Opening it at random I was soon into a story about a cold cure recommended by this chap on the bus— a cup of tea with garlic. It drew such a raucous a shriek of laughter from me that my next-door neighbour ran out, probably convinced that someone's throat was about to be slit.

I'd been given a copy of his book *Hermes and Magdalen* as birthday present from Michael, my husband, a month or two earlier. This volume, a silk bound, limited edition consisting of forty-three poems plus twenty etchings illustrating the theme of the God, the Goddess, the Mystical Marriage and the Magical Child, is a very different cup of tea from the Didymus selection, as you might gather, and, for some reason I can't remember clearly, we began corresponding from this point. Then it was I had this dream and acted, as some would see it, on impulse, though this kind of inner prompting often arises from a wiser place than that term implies. Thinking John might just be interested I included an account of it in a letter I sent to him.

John insists on writing his own letters by hand, inimitably idiosyncratic yet clearly and blackly. Although, thanks be, he accepts replies in nasty, common mechanical type. This excerpt from one such typed letter I sent him in reply to a hand-crafted page of his own recounts the dream.

July 2008

Dear John,
.... I'm going to tell you a dream I had a couple of weeks ago. I can hear you groan, and you have my full permission to ignore it if you want. However. Here goes!

I emerge from my cave close to the top of the mountain. Everything is white – ground permanently covered in snow. I look round at this familiar scene – my domain – beautiful black, skeletal trees sparkling with frost and sharp, diamond-glinting icicles. Everything is pure, no footprints, the air pristine. After breathing it in I make my way down to the village in the valley below, taking my time. After a while I see the Head Man of the village coming to meet me. He is an old friend and it seems we have an arrangement to meet regularly so he can consult me on all kinds of matters to do with the welfare of his people; spiritual, agricultural, health, family disputes, what-ever. I am aware at this point that I am male too, a shaman and storyteller.

The Head Man tells me he has become disturbed recently – he's had intimations – something not being quite right. At first it isn't clear what the problem is. We stand without speaking as though we're waiting for it to become clear. After a few moments he points to something lower down the mountain indicating he can sense where the trouble lies, yet neither of us can see what it is causing us both this concern. He turns towards me, meeting my eyes, and asks if I will go down there and take a look. Whatever it is he's sure it's something dangerous and that it's beginning to threaten the village in a serious way.

We shake hands and I take my leave of him and begin trekking down the pass to investigate. The pass steepens, grows narrower; it also begins to feel unusually warm with a certain familiar smell which

I can't put a name to. Then I stop, my body registering shock, as I come upon a mass of glittery black lava like a solidified river. It fills the steep gully almost to the top– choking it. Although I have only this minute discovered it, I know the black river has always been there, inert and unmoving, solid as rock, a feature of the landscape which I've been aware of all my life. I know too that neither in living memory nor in the folk memory of the tribespeople has it ever moved.

It came originally out from the bowels of the earth, from Gaia, and has been in this inert and passive state seemingly since the beginning of time – millions of years. But as I stand there observing intensely, trying to understand what it is that's threatening the villagers, the black tip of the flow higher up the gully begins creeping upwards. The whole mass has become pliable and warm, and its distinct smell, sulphurous, tarry, I now realise is the same I encountered on my way down without recognising it. I stand fascinated, mesmerised, wondering what it is all about, but now, as I watch, the speed of its flow increases. I turn and follow its progress upwards, aware now that it is heating up and rising towards my own cave. The fate of the village is set aside – this emergency is now my priority.

It strikes me that this lava flow is a reverse image of a glacier: a pure, white, frozen river, a glacier makes its way a fraction of an inch at a time, but naturally it moves downwards. This flow is curious in that this once inert, solidified black river is deciding to move upwards as if coming to life.

I quicken my steps to keep up, and am astonished to see that the leading edge of the lava is now shaping itself into an enormous beast – a dinosaur. I'm even more astonished when it divides, pairing off into two, and suddenly one creature, then the other comes to life as they struggle to free themselves from the black mass. They are quite clearly a male and a female pair, dragon-like, massive, heavy and immensely powerful. I'm horrified as I realise they're intent on reaching my cave, but there's a moment's relief because a high rock-face stands before them, stopping them.

But the sense of relief evaporates as quickly as it arrived, as terrified now, I watch these immense creatures filled with a blind primitive urge desperately trying to scale the rock. But having just emerged from their sleep of ages, it seems they're as unsteady as yolk-covered baby birds sprawling out of the egg. They don't yet have the skill or strength, in spite of their powerful claws, to climb up the escarpment and gain entry to my cave. But it won't be long before they manage it; they're gaining strength all the time.

I find myself now, as though for the first time, on the outside of my cave able to see into it. It's as though I've never viewed my dwelling place from this perspective before. I am surprised how very comfortable it looks inside. Not at all cave-like. It has all my precious belongings; my books, my art materials, my music collection, my stash of delicious food, not to mention my comfy sofa and chairs. Oh my God! I realise they're going to get in and smash it all up!

OK, this is where I wake up, John.

Back to the real world. I wonder if £10 will cover a further copy of the Didymus book?

Love, Esmé

I received this reply handwritten in thick black pen.

July 21st '08

Dear Esme,

Two for a tenner (you can leave one on a park bench.)

That's some dream! What suggests itself to me is opportunity for some culminative integration of the <u>animus</u>, the power aspect. In one way the thing that's not quite right! The petrified lava flow. If it were glacier/ice it would suggest to me 'frozen' pain; but the black lava is different, more earth, more of the dark feminine, more the feeling repressed because it is too hot to handle – and relating to the primordial, <u>massa confussa</u>, arrested, and now ready to be on the move. The 'enormous beast' seems to indicate the 'chthonic' primal force, and it now will find expression, and the power of it that could be all-destructive is wonderfully focussed by the 'coniunctio' of the dragons, the pair of them on the way up, on the way to consciousness, where a <u>right royal</u> coniunctio could be on the cards, even *if it requires a 'renewal' of the furnishings, a clear-out from the larder of those past-their-sell-by date jars, and a repositioning of the favourite sofa.*

But, of course, that may just be my dream!

Love, John

This, to my mind, has that Jungian flavour, and it sent me off to my dictionary to look up *chthonic*, a word I'd come across before in Jung's writings over the years. I love unusual words, and this was one of my favourites. I sort of knew what it meant but needed to refresh my understanding. It would have been hopeless to go plowing through the 'collected works' searching there in the hope of coming across it, hence the resort to my Pocket Oxford Dictionary. Blow me down if it didn't have it! It had 'ctenoid', if by any remote chance you're interested – but I wasn't, so I turned elsewhere to J. C. Cooper's Illustrated Encyclopaedia of Symbols, where under 'Dragons' I turned up – *'Dragons, as monsters, are autochthonous masters of the ground against which heroes, conquerors and creators must fight ...'* Ahha, I thought, this feels like we're getting somewhere! Then back to Jung himself, and in his *Psychology and Alchemy* I found – unearthed, perhaps a better word – that *'Dark = Chthonic, i.e. concrete, earthy; the prima materia; the Dangerous, Dark, Anima; the unconscious aspect of the Feminine ...'* which, and I'm paraphrasing now, needs to come into consciousness, and is activated by the Hero when he responds to the 'Call'. (Or on the contrary, if he ducks the Call out of fear then the Dark Feminine regresses and sets like 'concrete' in its negative sense.) I slid into paraphrasing here because at this point I'd opened yet another book – *The Writer's Journey*, by Christopher Vogler.

Vogler speaks of The Hero's Journey as 'The Call to Adventure.' So much of what he writes in his Epilogue seems directly related to this dream. The Hero is a man or woman who sets out on a journey to wholeness, to integration of all the parts and pieces which are not yet conscious. The unconscious aspects of gender, i.e. certain elements of the Feminine principle or the Masculine principle, are particularly in need of integration before we can become whole. I find it interesting personally that he says; *'Shamans have been called "the wounded healers" and like writers, they are special people set apart from the rest by their dreams, visions and unique experiences. The Hero's Journey and The Writer's Journey are one and the same... writing is magic... teaching children how to manipulate letters to make words: to spell. When you 'spell' a word correctly you are in effect casting a spell; ...charging these abstract symbols with meaning and power. Even the simplest act of writing is almost supernatural, on the borderline with telepathy... Shamans, like many writers, are prepared for their work by enduring terrible ordeals... They may have a dangerous illness or fall from a cliff and have every bone broken... They are taken apart and put together again in a new way.'*

It gave me goosepimples to read this because my very first book was written as a result of a serious illness which virtually paralysed me and put paid to the career I'd set my heart on. This illness forced me to give up sculpture which I'd specifically trained for and practised since leaving college in 1958, and in the most 'miraculous' way directed me to becoming a writer.

And the subtitle of that first book, Pathway Into Sunrise, was – *'Journey of a Wounded Healer'!*

All of this – goosebumps and all – had come out of John's wise and insightful comments. But how do *I* see my dream? Not in Freudian terms as you might have gathered. Freud, in his day, was a revolutionary thinker and a scientist. On the subject of religion he was in parallel with Karl Marx, another revolutionary thinker of the time, in pronouncing it an opiate of the people. And again I have some sympathy with these views. But did he make any attempt to distinguish religious beliefs with their organised systems of doctrine and dogma, from spiritual intelligence? Or even open himself to such a concept? As I said, the other Karl, Carl Jung, with whom Freud had a dramatic, not to say *traumatic* professional split, made, at great cost, his own important journey of discovery into that transpersonal part of the human psyche of which dreams are the communicating doorways.

The rift between the two pioneer psychoanalysts had come about, not only in the way each of them regarded the significance of dreams, but also over the publication of a book. As junior colleague to the more established Freud, Jung had set out his own understanding of the unconscious mind based on several years observation while working in the same Zurich mental health institution as his mentor. Jung saw Consciousness as rising from the dark and fertile depths of the Unconscious, whereas Freud asserted the opposite as being the case. Jung suspected him of being riled at having his authority questioned. But as later material reveals, Freud's equilibrium did seem to have been quite severely shaken as a result of the quarrel.

An important difference between the two men, yet one which I – perhaps the artist in me – finds attractive, is that Jung is often accused by his critics of being 'irrational,' thereby according Freud, with his rational, and more scientifically biased technique, superior status in the analytical hierarchy. An opinion, of course, with which many people concur. More than one client has been disconcerted and even angry in the presence of this warm and charming man, to find themselves faced, at one session, with Jung taking the opposite view of an issue from the one they'd been pursuing the previous week. But the kind of consistency of theory which they'd expected from a doctor of the mind, was not his way: 'going with the flow' to see where the moment led, although more risky, might reveal important blockages, but also surprising strengths or overlooked layers of beauty. Although many people in their insecurity look for a God-like father figure and a 'Law' to follow, he refused the mantle of authority. Instead he offered a more creative path to Wholeness, not a technique, but an individual encounter in which both could explore the dimensions of relationship. A relationship in which he would lay himself as open to shifts and turns, blind alleys and serendipitous discoveries as they. It was a journey they took together, mutually enriching.

Others have been dismayed, when perhaps discussing a dream, to have him suddenly go off on a reminiscence. For one client he recounted how another young woman in analysis had told him that she'd been walking on the moon the previous night. 'Surely you mean she dreamed it, imagined she was there?' the client responded. 'Oh no,' he said, looking her straight in the eye, 'It was real. She was *there*.'

Gradually, as they got to know him, they would realise that for him, dreams *were* reality. The truth that lay within the heart of myth, dreams and visions was a far greater reality than the 'stony desert' circling planet Earth.

Returning to my Shaman dream, what strikes me about that is how it poses – or juxtaposes – dramatic polar opposites; the intense whiteness against the equally intense blackness; cold against heat; the deepest level possible in that the black lava issues from the core of the Earth, and the pristine, crystalline whiteness at the mountain top where it touches 'the Heavens'. And then it gives us the Shaman, Healer and Storyteller, mediating between the two; Dark *v*. Light. Are they in opposition? In conflict? Are they posing a supreme danger to one another? Well maybe they *are* at the stage where the dream opens. If each exists in separation, unconscious of the other, out of communication, then perhaps that petrified state, (petrified by fear?) – the 'set in concrete' blackness and the static immovable icy whiteness – then as long as this state persists, Mother Earth's inhabitants *are* in danger. She, Gaia is also in danger, and this is where The Hero, the Healer, the one who makes Whole, must come in.

The Journey is before us:—

DREAMING WORLDS AWAKE

SYNCHRONICITY

The word Synchronicity was coined by Jung to describe meaningful coincidences occurring, for instance, when a dream, vision, or other inwardly perceived event corresponds to an event in external reality.

> 'The simultaneous occurrence of events appearing to be related but without apparent causal connection ....' Ruth White
>
> *Divine Timing; Communing with Spirit.*   Esmé Ellis

Fifteen years ago, when I first began to write, the Internet was a vague unknown territory I hardly thought about, never mind dipped my toes in. (Does one dip toes into territory?) Yet by the time my third book, *This Strange and Precious Thing*, was launched in September 2008, it had become an established field of communication for millions of people all over the world, enabling we humans to meet one another in ways formerly undreamed of. Yet, rather like human nature itself, it turned out to be a two-sided coin. Nevertheless, good thing or bad, a network of potentials had been created which people lost no time exploring and exploiting. On the positive side, and one possibility which interested me, was that it began to present new ways for writers and artists to publish and promote their stuff.

There has always been a field of consciousness operating outside the physical form of things, and various ways too in which people who've sensed it or encountered aspects of it have described it; collective unconscious, the unified field, morphic resonance, the astral sphere, the ethereal.... But until recently there have been rather few proficient enough to use this field for clear and reliable communication. However, for good or ill, we're where we are; we're here: this is the New Era. And it's my belief, that if we allow ourselves to go beyond the mind, develop a new intelligence which relies less on our old stand-by the intellect, with its logical reasoning and analysis as our primary organ of understanding and gathering information, of creating, then the more easily we shall learn to surf these oceanic fields.

The Internet is a model of these fields. It is both a manifestation and an extension of Human Consciousness; its speed of communication reflects the growing interconnectedness of us all. Human ingenuity and technology today is wonderful: it has brought us to a place never before known or dreamed of, and promises to take us further afield and faster still – to who knows where. As we leave behind old ways of doing things, the laborious, the slow and cumbersome, we can honour the grace and beauty, the skill and dedication that went into some of those creations which served us so wonderfully down the ages. But as people at the leading edge begin to create new pathways of consciousness, even our smart technology is superseded by increasingly less material-based systems. I see the 'top of the mountain' in my Shaman dream symbolically as both launch pad and touch down, a place where the Sacred Self meets the earth-bound human self. There, human intelligence meets Divine Intelligence, and Synchronicity is just one of the mysterious connective forces which arise from this encounter. *Notice me*, it demands, *and I will respond with further revelations.*

* * *

VIEW OVER ATLANTIS

The book launch for *This Strange and Precious Thing* had come and gone in the Autumn, and now, Friday, towards the end

DREAMING WORLDS AWAKE

of February, I was preparing some last minute publicity to pin up for the "Great Waterstone's Signing Event" the following day.' I'd printed out a couple of posters with pictures and reviews, also some sheets for people to take away. Then planned an afternoon nap. But I'd woken feeling disorientated, groggy from the effects of a lingering virus.

It had been a miserable winter one way or another, and I catch colds, though not like other people's colds. Mine are 5 to 6 week affairs and worse than any flu I've personally experienced. I have a persistent cough anyway, a winter, spring and summer irritant visitor, but with a cold this flares into uncontrollable spasms of such intensity that my throat seizes up completely, throttling me so I can't draw breath. These episodes also involve a full-speed dash to the loo with a bucket. The details when I don't get there in time I leave to your imagination.

To say I'd been pleased when the Bath manager invited me before Christmas to do this Signing is to understate it somewhat, but now the day itself – along with this darned cold – was on top of me, I was just a smidge worried. They'd given me a table in a prominent position on the ground floor where, the idea was, people would wander up eager to talk about the book. Talking, I knew from painful experience, sets off this cough, and Waterstone's loo was on the floor above, and not even a lift. The thought of engaging customers in a series of riveting conversations over a period of three hours was making me nervous. Too late to cancel, or so I told myself, I'd just have to listen to My Friends in Higher Places and trust myself to the moment.

Shakily, in the wake of the snooze, I made my way downstairs trying to focus on 'tasks in hand'; check emails, see if anything importantly last minute had come in, add final touches to posters and info. Halfway down the stairs I remembered that, just before drifting off to sleep I'd seen a vague figure at the foot of the bed. He was sitting there, his hands holding my feet, giving me healing. I continued unsteadily down the last few steps and made my way to my work corner. I switched on the laptop and waited while the Yahoo 'Breaking News' items settled so I could go to my mail page. I don't bother to read Yahoo news, but on this occasion my eye was caught; an item which hadn't been there earlier, headed, *Has The Lost City of Atlantis Been Found?*

I'd been promised a write-up in the *Bath Chronicle* in good time for the Signing. The Art Editor told me he'd meant to include it two weeks ago, but there'd been heavy snow, roads suddenly impassable and all kinds of hold-ups as a result. They couldn't find room for it. It wasn't there the following week either. Too late now, I thought, to have any impact on the Signing. Nevertheless I bought myself the latest edition. Once more I hunted through all the local doings and goings on without spotting my write-up, and was convinced they'd dropped me again – then I finally saw it. My initial disappointment blossomed into surprise as I slowly took in the implications. The delay had landed me on the same page as the Bath Literary Festival Book Reviews – quite prominently, with a decent picture of the cover. I was in good company!

With shameless inattention to the illustrious authors reviewed above me, I turned to my write-up at the foot of the page. One paragraph was headed; *The Island which Plato claimed to be the last remaining tip of lost Atlantis, is the setting for this many-layered story.*' I'd already used this quote on one of my posters, and now on the computer screen before me was this Yahoo News headline! I clicked on the full story and hastily printed it out in economy black and white. What a gift! I could use it – flag up Breaking News – on my publicity. It even had a picture, a deep ocean map of the exact site placed just where I'd set my story; an island in the Atlantic Ocean off the coast of North Africa.

I crossed the room looking for a folder to put it in safe for tomorrow, then hesitated. 'Black and white economy, meany? If it's for your poster why don't you do it in full colour?' I went back to the laptop and stared at the page. The news item had gone! Lost Atlantis had disappeared! If I hadn't opened it up at precisely that moment only a couple of minutes ago *I wouldn't have seen it!*

Next day the Signing went well. My cold mysteriously cleared up, and there'd been quite some interest in the Atlantis connection: at least it had been a talking point. Now I was left wondering why it had drawn itself to me in this strange, not to say uncanny, manner. Maybe the word, synchronicity, as defined by its author Jung, was shifting to include a wider definition of my own. Yet these external events and the timing of their occurrence had to be more than mere coincidence. The Island, deliberately unnamed, but located at the spot which Plato referred to as the last remaining tip of Lost Atlantis, was the setting for, as well as an important theme in the book. Various characters in the story argue about its existence. Annya, a present-day sceptic, scoffs when the question of its reality comes up, while for Finn, my character from the future, Atlantis is unquestionably fact. Not able to come down on one side or the other, I as author declare myself open-minded, but treat it more as a myth. Are all the characters that we create parts of ourselves? I was left wondering. Was I Annya the sceptic, the author sitting on the fence, or more in tune with Finn than I dared to admit? These questions still hanging on the air I let the subject drop.

* * *

But that wasn't to be the end of it. A few weeks later, another nap, another eye-blinking flash from Up-There! (and even more questions about just who is it up there creating these synchs? Yet another part of myself, maybe!)

SYNCHRONICITY

In *This Strange and Precious Thing,* Annya is in the grip of a mild breakdown after finding herself alone on The Island facing a series of bewildering phenomena. She'd gone there on holiday with journalist Simon, her older brother's closest friend, but when he's called away on a secret assignment, suddenly, it seems, someone – or perhaps some*thing* has broken into their apartment. Inexplicable events escalate as she searches for help and reassurance, but her new-found friends only bring further unsettling situations. The theme of Atlantis runs through the book, and the idea that this Lost Continent is anything but a myth is just one of the many crazy and other-worldly possibilities she is struggling with as her grip on reality slips away.

I don't pretend to have any great insights into Atlantean civilisation. Others have spoken about the subject and thrown out various theories and so-called facts, but until now, I've been happy to call myself open-minded on the subject. However I am growing increasingly uncomfortable at the number of co-incidences which are beginning to cluster around me. That looming sculpture in the corner of my room – the one I made over thirty years ago of an enthroned figure crowned with the priest-like head-dress – it's watching me. Is he an Atlantean from my past? What is he trying to tell me?

I was turning this and other thoughts over in my mind – having a conversation with myself – or this other part of myself. Could I have once been that very priest of Atlantis? That figure I'd sculpted and who sits now in judgement, staring, immobilised and welded to his chair? What a notion. What a load of cobblers. What evidence have you anyway – or for that matter what has anyone come up with in the way of actual proof that Atlantis ever existed?

A voice, this other part of myself, presumably, started speaking. 'But you've just turned up some evidence. Why do you think you opened that old notebook, the one you'd

DREAMING WORLDS AWAKE

forgotten about; the one you took out a few days ago when you decided it was time to sort out your shelves and see what needed throwing away? Why did it open at that particular page, the diary page? Straight from the horse's mouth, don't you think? Your very own on-the-spot report of your first day on The Island, and how you took a trip out to the 'firefields' which you later used in your book; your very own description of how, that evening when you were back in the apartment resting, eyes closed, you began to see yourself flying over the black volcanic wastes. There, in your own words, your record of what you saw – all those incredible colours flying out; those wonderful blues, violets, magentas, purples, greens and mysterious amber-golds and silvers, streaming out from the jet-black ground, non-stop for over an hour. What was that if not evidence of lost Atlantis beneath you?'

'That's all very well,' I said, arguing with this other self, 'but you can't count that as evidence.' Pushing my thoughts, my voices, away, I stood up. 'Time for for a cuppa,' I told myself, 'and then better get on with some work.' On my way to the kitchen I absent-mindedly switched on the radio. Radio 4. An interesting speaker caught my attention. I walked on past my laptop which I turned on ready to resume work. Still listening I went into the kitchen and switched on the kettle, still listening, the sound following me all the way. John Michell, said the radio voice, a New Age writer – *'Huh! never heard of him'* – his books from the 60s and 70s – *'Yeh. OK.'* Flying Saucers and ley lines. *'How very New Age!'* I muttered scornfully. And his most famous book of all, the radio voice continued, a cult book which influenced such luminaries as Mick Jagger, Keith Richards, Marianne Faithfull along with The Rolling Stones and Pink Floyd – and its title; *'The View Over Atlantis'*. 'Oh!' – And then, in a moment of inspired timing, the music began to pour from the radio. A track from one of those albums.... **'She comes in colours everywhere. Streaming colours everywhere. Combing colours from her hair.'**

25

CYBERSPACE

1/ CONNECTING

This is my fantasy: the world, teeming with friends and lovers,
eager to find me, as I am to discover them. We reach out,
fingertip-touching, strangers exploring strangely,
outwardly, inwardly. Faces, thoughts, beating hearts, minds;
oceans of consciousness through which we cast our lines;
great seas which know no barriers – except,
those we have built – fortresses to withstand
such golden-eyed and alien what-may-bees.

'This is Good Ship Virtuality. You're adrift,
dreaming The Impossible into being.
That's stupid,' you say. 'For the birds. If God
had meant us wings... that's impossible.
No-one believes such things.'

Exactly! There you have it: that's a wall.
We build them all the time – these walls – invest
in bricks and mortar. Foundations of civilization,
that's what these are. Our Citadel, built to last.
Our true belief inside which we shelter, towered
and turreted. It must not fail. Nor fall.

Yet, will it? Might not this Otherness –
this unbounded and uncertain encounter we seek –
be just the catalyst which will open gates
in our imprisoned minds?

Will it: and it will.
Only connect – only dream the dream,
and Berlin Walls tumble,
ideologies crumble,
Dawn's trumpets call.

30-11-08

DREAMING WORLDS AWAKE

2/ PROFILES

Idealised hope and naïve trust
comes to grieving soon as must,
floundering in mutual distrust,
deceits and misperception.
Relationship's a two-side coin,
one's true gold, the other's rust.

You share your face, it smiles at me,
but who you are I cannot see
what lurks behind that groomed I.D.
Your history's fine, your C.V's pat,
but how I wonder what you're at.
In all of this, oh cyberfriend,
wherein lies reality?

18-10-09

3/ THE WEB

I journeyed – setting out towards you, stranger, alight
with my innocent hope, yet already I'm in a twisted corridor
of polished glass and whispers. Mirror surfaces reflecting
distortion bounce back with unbalanced resonance. Why then?

My greeting and my smile, open like my hand,
a palm for meeting yours, declares, 'no concealed weapons.'
Why then? When this was meant to be so simple,
why this distrust of purpose?
You show me your hand, and it's a fan of spread cards, but
like an opening gambit. I listen for your meaning, and hear
only the meaning of The Game and the ghost behind the glass,
lost in the eddies and whorls of empty sound.
You're playing your cards well. *My* hand's no match.

This face, which greeted yours with honest smiling, contorts,
falsely skewed upon the surface of your mind, turning me inside out.
My intention betrayed, I turn away, but the corridor twists again,
spinning gilded lures and charms of fine fabrication; dewy nets
laced with honey sweetness. My breath snatches at the thin, overheated air.
My heart's pulse grasps a fistful of breath sensed on a faraway breeze.

CYBERSPACE

Trapped, my urgent feet, now streaked with a blur of speed-lines,
race towards phantom exits down this Whispering Gallery.

23-04-09

4/ HOME PAGE

Stranger, you come forward, toward me.
But what is it you carry in your greeting?
Assumptions, conclusions, opinions,
or a simple open door and Welcome mat?
Then the question: How do you see me,
taste me, touch me? What senses and
sensibilities do you bring to the encounter?
Without doubt you're a Woman of the World, like me.
With what suspicion and wariness do you
observe the manner I enter your house?

This street mud you've noticed caking my feet,
betrays, perhaps, some darker turns my own path
took on the way to your door. Does your threshold
message, that rough-coated Welcome mat,
have a shaman's power to wipe clean, absolve?
But I see you've already put the kettle on.

Graciously you accept my flower-gift offering
which you bring to your face to smell:
and now, breathing in as you arrange it,
distributing stalks and leaves;
displaying blossoms in your mind as you dip
its thirsty stems into the pitcher full of water.
That crystal draught of cool transparency,
sang to me of its high-land birth as you drew it
from the common-place tap in your kitchen: This kitchen,
this Common Place, this Home where we quench our thirst.
We're there at last. Home at last. Home from Home.

07-05-09

STORIES

ABOUT A TORTOISE

I was at Uyune Sanhaja. I'd gone there on a last-minute-out-of-the-blue holiday. Just four days. A lifetime all packed into a mini-break capsule. Uyune Sanhaja is a historic Arabic house or riad, or rather one of a complex of riads under reconstruction. The section we were to stay in along with the extensive garden and pool had been fully renovated, but the rest were still in a long-neglected state of dilapidation or in process of being restored. I too was in process of being restored.

The journey to Morocco had been long and tiring; setting off late afternoon Thursday, almost four hours stop-over at Casablanca and a delayed plane meant we didn't arrive at Uyune Sanhaja until around two-thirty a.m. Friday. But even in the dark chill of the late night/early morning air the welcome was warm, and from what we could see of it the place itself was magnificent. As we were shepherded across mosaic tiles through a series of courtyards and terraces with ornately carved canopies and barley-sugar pillars, we caught, between the branches of mulberry trees hung about with twinkling lights, glimpses of a crescent moon in the garden pool. Then, as we were ushered through yet another magnificently carved door to our escort's whispered 'Voilà. Here are your rooms,' the magic of an Arabian Night began to sink in for real.

Our twin apartments stood on either side of an inner courtyard. Two great glass and bronze double doors faced each other across a spacious blue and white marble floor set about with sofas and deep arm chairs. And all of this – was 'our apartment!' Luxurious bed, traditional Fessi rugs, more soft chairs round a pearl inlaid table upon which bowls of exotic fruits and sweetmeats were set out. Another carved door to one side was opened to reveal a state-of-the-art toilet with hand-held spray for thorough cleansing. Then across to the door opposite where a sunken, turquoise mosaic-tiled shower with silver filigree fittings completed the picture. With all this as starters, what possibly might follow?

I can't say I had any specific expectations right then. Alone at last and travelling clothes doffed and folded, I stretched out on silken sheets and sank back into a pile of pillows. Barely registering the carved and painted ceiling through the canopy of the four-poster bed I slid into sleep. If there'd been thoughts at all in my mind they must have been a vague desire to spend the whole of the next day lazing and recuperating, leaving my two companions to do their own thing.

The sun had been out to greet us as we'd dawdled over a late breakfast next morning on the terrace. Wanting to make the most of their four days Dhevi and Marc had decided on a trip to the Atlas Mountain villages, and I was lying in the shade by the pool when Rosa, the delightful lady who'd escorted us to our rooms in the dark, came to say 'hi'. We chatted comfortably. Can't remember about what. I felt relaxed. I was being taken care of. Discreetly at intervals she came and went, brought big soft towels for my swim, told me I could order anything, have a salad lunch, mint tea or something more dangerously alcoholic if preferred. I was feeling my way into being in a Muslim country the first time in my life, and this, I reminded myself, was Friday. Calls to prayer drifted up from the Medina. I pottered around and made friends with a straggly haired Labrador who'd been for a swim in the pool. Apart from the dog, I had the fresh spring water to myself.

DREAMING WORLDS AWAKE

Late afternoon, I asked Rosa how the restoration project was coming on. She said she'd show me. We wandered down between lavender and Saint Helena borders and crossed the garden by the lower path past the dog now snoozing under an old Indian swing. Slobbering with delight he straightened up and shook himself sending saliva and water drops everywhere. He must have been for a dip again. I took photos of craftsmen at work in the buildings where panels of amazingly skilful decorative carving was in process, then decided to sample that mint tea. As the afternoon restfully progressed towards evening we shifted my lounger into more shade, and I leaned back. Sounds and scents gently merged wafting me into a reverie-cum-meditation. My program of restoration was going smoothly. Paradise, I reflected, was originally a pleasure garden for nobles and Persian Kings – and I was allowing myself a taste of Paradise on Earth.

I was abruptly shot back to the here and now by a cold, wet weight on my left foot. I registered a sensation of scaly pads of skin and claws. Wet dogs foot! Friendly this old mutt might be, I thought, but wasn't this taking friendship a bit far? Didn't he know about startling a person in the midst of her private inner experience? My eyes wide open now were staring at my foot, upon which, and staring right back at me, was a tortoise. I tipped him off with a shudder – and instantly felt ashamed of myself for my reaction.

Next evening, tempted, not to say intrigued, by our host's suggestion of a whisky nightcap in their bar, (a drink which in fact turned out to be Dry Martini; the bottle's label disporting an alcoholic calibration had fed the assumption that somehow all liquorous substances haling from the West are whiskey), we accepted the invitation and explored the heights of the upper floors. Rosa and Idriss our host joined us. Our chosen tipples, non-alcoholic or otherwise, in hand, the whole of Fez, a black carpet encrusted with stars, spread out below, we became engrossed in a stimulating conversation – philosophy, the concept of Divine Unity, Islamic art and design, World Music and literature. Rosa, it transpired, had 'looked me up' before our arrival and informed Idriss I was a writer. The usual polite query; What kind of writer? What kind of book? I tried to explain. Not altogether successfully. But my explanations never are. Yet they seemed interested enough, and with some enthusiasm recommended in return, *Momo*, a children's book by Michael Ende in which both were sure I would find similarities to my own work. I think I must have frowned. I hope I hadn't offended them but I don't consider myself a children's author. Nevertheless by now I'd learned enough respect for them to ask for details before we reluctantly set off for the airport a couple of days later.

Now, this is where it gets interesting – or so it seem to me. I bought the book and started reading it soon after reaching home.

* * *

Momo is a little girl, a ragged waif with enormous insight and simplicity and a magical gift for storytelling. People, especially hordes of local children, are drawn to her, and not only by her captivating fantasies, but even more by her gift of listening. Young and old alike come with their problems only to find that in her presence their own creativity and imagination spring to life. Unaccountably they go away again having understood and solved the very thing that troubled them. But then – and there's always a 'but then' in magical stories – things begin to go awry. I won't spoil it by giving more away except to say that when 'things' seem at their darkest and most terrifying, two new characters appear;

the mysterious Professor Hora and his strangely gifted tortoise, Cassiopeia. Her gift is an uncanny ability to view the future and convey crucial fore-knowledge by manifesting messages on her shell. And how do you think Cassiopeia announces her presence to Momo on each and every occasion? ***By standing on her left foot!***

This might be seen as coincidence: it might have prompted Rosa to think of telling me about the book – if not consciously, then possibly unconsciously. That is if I had told her about the incident with the tortoise on my foot.

Thing is though – Why did that tortoise decide to announce itself to me that way?

> Kuthumi: *Ah your tortoise....when you tell me these stories I remember my time as St Francis of Assisi. I was so in tune with nature because I had opened up my energies beyond the simple limits of the physical world. I felt into the energies of animals and they responded by communicating with me as easily as I spoke with another person. They would come to me to share news of newborns or would know I would provide refuge if they needed it. It was a wonderful energy to be in .... and taught many of the nature of being spiritual in a time when that was restricted by laws and rules of the church. This energy ties in with your energy of reflection in your dream....because when we choose to reflect and open parts of us up....then more energies can resonate with us. For St Francis and you...this is with animals. So your tortoise led you to a book which was to essentially show you how the energies of writing can combine with teaching in a new way. Now this communication is something you can choose to expand more....but truly keep it light and fun. Do not go looking for these connections with the animals. They will come and they will find you...and they will be magic...*

Kuthumi Lal Singh is an Ascended Master, and oh, what a joy and privilige to include his comments here under the heading of Correspondences. I shall say more of him later, but for now :— The story unfolds...

DIDO

Some time later, back home, developments have been taking place for me. Journeys into Cyberspace, new contacts, more writings, new poems, new consciousness, new energies, new awareness, more dreams, further synchronicities. Magic, it seems is becoming an everyday reality.

A dialogue develops between my Here on Earth self and My Self on other – higher, if you like – planes of reality. Also a dialogue between myself down here in the linear time-bound and physical world and the aforementioned Master Kuthumi on the 'other side of the veil.' As these new dialogues and cyber-conversations unfold, so do my dreams spell out their own stories. We've looked at the derivation of the word, *spell*? Words themselves have magic. They cast spells. They have power – power to bind; power to free. How much more so then do communications beyond words.

As well as my adventures into cyberspace and things intangible, at a more mundane level I'd decided it was time for The Big Clean and Clear Out, and ever since my return from Morocco I've been throwing out loads of old stuff. Hard going both physically and emotionally as it included work I'd held in huge folders under the bed. There were drawings and photos of sculptures, stuff which had been carefully mounted dating from years ago when I applied for the two top London colleges at the end of my time as a student at the Sheffield College of Art. There was also work I submitted when I applied for travelling scholarships and exhibitions after I left the London college and launched myself out on what I hoped would be 'my brilliant career' as an artist. Now, sixty years later, I decided to throw it out –

recycle or burn it. '*Perfect!*' said Kuthumi. '*Let it all go and create some New Energies, New Works of Art.*'

I'd had the carpets cleaned, but instead of freshness, there's been this dank, musty sort of smell coming from under one particular rug right under my feet where I do my work. It wasn't there before – at least if it had been I'd never noticed.

Then I had this series of dreams: –

MORE DREAMS

There I sit at my laptop in my work corner, this curious smell issuing from under the carpet. I feel uneasy, not to say a bit scared. Something, it seems, is about to emerge, something shadowy, perhaps dangerous. But whatever it is – and as the dream flows on IT seems to be developing a personality – I want to call it Dido. The whole of the emerging image, subject and background, is vague and intangible at first. But as I stay with the name Dido, puzzling about it, it is as if the entity with that name is asking me what it means to me. 'It's like Momo,' I say. It's a little girl.' I wake here and go on puzzling about what it could mean.

* * *

Then, a few nights later I have another dream. I dream it *twice!* I realise right in the midst of the dream when it comes around the second time that I'd dreamed it the previous night at least once and forgotten it. So it must be important for it to keep on repeating.

I'm looking down the left hand side of a long corridor. All the way down are booths – small cubicles partitioned off. Gradually the impression emerges that I'm at an exhibition with displays by individual artists, but from where I'm standing I can only see a little of the work inside the first one.

In fact all I can see of that is a sculpted portrait mounted on the wall facing me. It's coming clear now that these booths contain displays of students' work, so it must be an end of term show, and this exhibition is crucial; it will determine their final qualifications. Then suddenly I recognise the portrait. It's a fellow student I knew at the College in London.

At that moment a little girl comes out of the booth. She's the image of the portrait. I'm delighted, so I tell her excitedly that I know her. But she shakes her head. Puzzled at this, and disappointed, I tell her, but if *you* don't know *me*, it must have been your mother I knew because you're so like her. She shakes her head again. I know this is a true recognition and I can't let it go at that – something strange is happening here and I want to get to the bottom of it. So I beckon her to me, remembering I didn't manage to make this gesture in the first dream. Maybe this is why the dream is presenting me with a new opportunity. I take a step towards her and, by this action I feel sure now that I've made a necessary change in my own energy. By taking this step I've moved beyond where I stood when I dreamed this before. It has opened me up to her: no longer at a distance I can now make a heart-to-heart relationship.

Now she comes towards me smiling, warm and friendly in spite of our rather uncertain start, and I feel her reality, see her much more clearly. She seems to trust me and a real relationship is blossoming. I tell her I am sure I actually knew her mother and that her name was Sue. But the little girl tells me quite clearly that neither her name not her mother's is Sue.

At this point I wake up still partly in the dream, puzzling it over. The dream is still with me, resonating as if it's playing with me – joking even – some part of myself having fun because it knows the answer, but asking me to follow the clues. It takes some time before the 'penny drops' and I realise that the person I knew was actually male and his name was Syd.

I'm so excited by this that I want to show Michael, my husband, a picture I still have in ARC, an old College magazine, of a piece of sculpture by this Sydney Harpley. It's a life-sized figure of a little girl sitting on a box near the ground. So now I have a fix on this little girl, although I still don't understand the reason for the male/female switch I decide to see what happens next.

* * *

ANOTHER DREAM

Some sort of transit station – a lot of commotion and confusion. As I settle into the scene, looking round, I begin to take in that it's some big concourse in a train station – people sitting on seats, waiting … and gradually I become aware that I am a little girl. At first I'm seeing her, watching her, but later I *am* her. As part of the crowd she is confused and bewildered, wandering about. Then as my sense of being there as The Observer clarifies I see that she is a Displaced Person.

There were many D. P.s at the end of the Second World War, and back when I was a student in Sheffield not long after the war finished, I had done a piece of sculpture – two spindly young girls leaning against each other for support.

As part of our recent domestic Big Clear Out on which Kuthumi had commented how good it was to let go old stuff and create new energies in my life, Michael had discovered me struggling to pull five heavy work folders from under the bed, and given me a hand. He helped to vacuum inches of dust off them, so I could sort through them before taking them down to the garden incinerator. I wanted a chance to have a last look and to say goodbye before throwing them on the funeral pyre. Images from so long ago brought bittersweet memories and tears to my eyes. Among the paintings and sculptures was a photo of my spindly girls, and I showed it to Michael, explaining how I'd made it just after the war because of being so very moved by the plight of children all over Europe who'd lost everything; their parents, family, homes. Many had been taken away and transported thousands of miles and put into concentration camps. They were thin and starving and had been victims and witnesses of enormous horror. As well as this piece of sculpture, I'd made these scenes the subject of a number of paintings around that time. I was drawn back into the same feelings of empathy, and letting go wasn't easy.

***

Cutting back to this dream at the rail station I seemed to be one of these children, except that although lost, displaced, I wasn't traumatised. I was objectively detached, watching myself amid the confusion: there for some reason. Knowing that if I trusted myself to the moment I would be taken care of whatever might happen.

I became aware of the need to 'spend a penny' and shyly went up to a figure in the crowd, a man sitting in the waiting area, and told him I needed to go to the lavatory, but didn't know where to find it. I didn't know the language either and couldn't read the public signs. I had no idea where I was or where I was going. This man was a young priest, Islamic, or maybe a Catholic priest. But he looked more Islamic with his long, light coloured robe and beard. He smiled and said he would take me there. He was very sensitive and considerate, and took me right to the door of the cubicle, and then returned to where he'd been sitting. I went in and sat on the seat and with a great relief did a lot of pee. It occurred to me that what had happened was very unusual. Normally this type of man, a religious figure, would not have dared, with all eyes upon him, to escort a little girl to the ladies' loo, never mind take her in. It made me feel this was a special sort of man; someone with great integrity who I could trust, someone who is able to rise above the 'false' doctrines of his religion which forbid a male to involve himself in such a 'dicey' situation. Just to test him out, to satisfy myself that he could be trusted, I got up from the loo and looked out of the door, then went back again. I left the door open allowing him to see in. He glanced up, assured himself I was okay sitting on the loo, then just went on calmly reading his book.

* * *

I am speculating now on the significance of the little girl's appearance – what is actually happening here.

Kuthumi: *The priest was me .... I came to reassure you and show you that things can change. This sense of displacement is this part of you still finding its way ... that's why I was happy to help you and take you to the loo ... so glad that in your dream you know how to release what you don't need inside you.*

Yes, right at the beginning of the scene I'd used the words, 'transit station'. I was in a place of transition. That's what the dream was telling me. But transit to what? Or where? This is why dreams are so fascinating to me: they're like a drama being played out in instalments.

DREAM INTO A POEM

This poem takes as its theme Blackness and Night and addresses our common fears around darkness. It conjures a magical and shamanic journey into the dark side where 'bats see fine'; (a somewhat imperfect allusion to Blind Captain Cat in Dylan Thomas's *Under Milk Wood*). Bats are symbolic of Birth, Death and Rebirth in some native cultures. The Shamanic journey typically takes us into and through the death experience with all its anxieties around confronting our own death. We experience, whilst still in this life, the necessary 'letting go' of the ego identity, a surrender which heralds rebirth. The Rockabye rhythm in the tree-tops in the last verse echoes not only the cradle, but the rocking motion of the ocean with its invitation to go beyond the Sound. That, fear it or welcome it, is the call to venture across the frontier separating the Known from the Great Unknown, this boundless and undefinable water out of which we may snatch a rare gleam or catch a spark to ignite a transformation in our lives.

CLIMBING WITH DIDO

This amazing child, alone, has survived, walked maybe a thousand miles, and now she stands before me, inviting me, holding out her hand. 'Come !' she says, 'Let's explore this garden.'

It's night and the only light is from the windows of a large villa, a rather grand country house built in the Italian manner. She leads me along a paved terrace overhung with wisteria and pale clustered roses. We walk past pools where lilies float on water ruffled by splashes cascading from lion heads and other strange half-animal, half-human faces. But soon we're climbing a path, where, as we tread higher, the house lights dwindle and fade, and the pavings under foot become more uneven. We continue up hand-in hand, and I let her lead me into the deepening, moonless darkness.

She knows where she wants to go. After all, having made her way to me over the years and over all these miles, I can certainly trust her direction and her sure-footedness now. And truly, even though we can barely see the ground, I have no difficulty walking alongside her. I realise where she is heading; she names it Dido's Temple.

Once inside I have glimpses of a connection with a remote mountain area close to Afghanistan. I see myself in a classroom with a group of adult students from several different countries. Many wear beards and sandals and are dressed in Arabic robes. We're doing an exercise together, choosing colours to talk about, except we can't speak each other's language. But somehow this exchange of choosing colours, very strange, unusual, rather special colours which we all comment on, brings about a lively and very warm friendship. We seemed to understand one another perfectly without the need of words.

We move onto another exercise, picking small pieces of coloured glass. These are even more unusual and difficult to define – colours beyond the usual range we' re used to, but extremely beautiful. They're actually like tiny lenses because when you look through them something remarkable happens. I hold one up. Gazing through it brings strange new experiences into focus. Not only am I able to see in a new way, but the lens seems to be drawing towards me a distant student. He's approaching down a corridor, but in this new light which the new colour sheds all around him, I see in a way I've never been aware of before, as though I read more deeply and compassionately the whole being of the person, rather than just gather superficial impressions.

Kuthumi: You have just re-experienced your time as a magus. You studied with me in times past, and we often gathered from all over Persia and Babylon (and yes this would have covered Afghanistan). So you can imagine the language barrier.. but we knew that that was no obstacle if we chose ways to communicate beyond words and in a universal way, that is; colours.

The Dido poem stems from that dream.

INCANTATION FOR DIDO

In this blackest of nights who guides:
who holds, and who supports whom?
Feeling the unsteady steps with our feet,
craze-cracked, with moss and fern between,
our eyes pitch blind, we climb without Moon,
yet know, as if with eyes that cannot
see, our destination.

Darkly I mark a terrace high above, antique
and marble paved. There, candle-lit within my
mind, are white clothed tables, ribbon laid with
stars of wine-filled crystal bowls, and voices wind in
limpid streams, through and in between herbed hedges.
Soon dancing feet we'll see trip light and fleet
along this Colonnade.

I turn from the stony path, breathing hard,
to short-cut up a sloping sward, my sightless
eyes urging me on; higher, faster – steeper.
But she cautions, touching my hand; tells
me without words, so I understand which
is the one. It's She who leads, this child
who came as stranger.

I see my role is to protect, and feel her shiver.
Her hand's cold as night's dew, and I wrap my arms
round her thinness. My mouth moves close to her ear;
Warmth, I murmur. *Warmth I must give you.* She points:
We must go up, she says, *Can't you hear, we're invited.*
Now in shadows, half way on, a house appears.
Ahh, she says, *that's Dido's Temple.*

DREAMING WORLDS AWAKE

Within this cloistered space we sit; *Come close,* I say,
and take her hand to stroke her blood back in. But
here's warmth enough already! Firelight glances off pillars
as if by magic, present too. And overhead, criss-crossed with
trailing stems for roof, one central, oriental lantern hangs,
soft, yet radiant with jewelled lozenges of glass.
We're bathed in gentle coloured light, and find —

Our feet glide smoothly on that marble terrace floor.
The feast now laid for all who care to join the dance.
The cloth spreads out, a river, white with spangled pools
where reflections spill blood-red from tall-stemmed flutes,
and garnet stains our fingers as we drink, and basking
in our own generated light, drink in the night. Till out
from leaf-dense boughs beneath, a swoop of skin-winged

Shadows dart, and scoop us up to tree-tops high where bats see fine.
Tops and tips, pitch black pitch and toss, we hear them sighing
rockabye – and night wraps us in her gentle arms. Beyond
the sound, behind the Moon, its tide is out beyond the Sound.
Tossed there and back again – but where – and will it be the same?
This witching night. Or when we wake. And oh, what difference
will it make? And difference shall we find this time? And will we
care – and shall we dare?

ANOTHER STORY = AND MORE CORRESPONDENCE

A word about Kuthumi here, and how it was we came to engage in this series of dialogues.

I spoke earlier about finding new ways of meeting people on the internet – new pathways of consciousness and communication. Marisa Calvi lives in Australia. She had created on her website, www.newenergywriting.com a space which she called Creators Playground. Intrigued, I contacted her. Right away she invited me 'to play', and I did an on-line interview with her in June 2009. She too had just published a book featuring a story told to her directly by Kuthumi Lal Singh.

Kuthumi has gained great knowledge and insight into human experience from his many lifetimes which have included incarnations as Balthasar, Pythagoras, St. Francis of Assisi, and Shah Jahan who built the Taj Mahal, and in the 1800's as Mahatma Koot Hoomi Lal Singh working with Madame Blavatsky to form the Theosophical Society.

He'd appeared to Marisa one night in her hotel bedroom where she was attending a Crimson Circle conference in Colorado. 'Good, you're awake,' he'd said. She knew he was due to speak, channelled by Geoffrey Hoppe, at the conference next morning, but this late night appearance in the bedroom took her by surprise. 'I've written some stories, he announced later as they seated themselves downstairs, and I'm looking for someone to help me tell them to the world?' Marisa had already been thinking of writing a book and the timing of this opportunity was uncannily perfect. So she agreed.

This book was meant to be a first short volume covering his lifetime as Thutmose III, Pharaoh of Egypt in BC 1465 but grew to over 440 gripping pages.

After my interview appearance on Marisa's Playground, I took up a further invitation to pose a few questions to Kuthumi. There were indeed questions, personal and troubling, which I'd longed to put to someone with his level of wisdom and insight. I e-mailed off my first one, and I had this reply back from Marisa:

> Sorry I'm a bit behind writing this up for you. I got the bulk of this session last night and then it abruptly stopped! I usually allow a follow-up e-mail for people who need some clarity on what is written or if it opens up something else, but Kuthumi has said to 'open up a dialogue with you'. …. Namaste, Marisa.

So that was how it began:–
And this is a story which arose out of those sessions.

BLACKBIRD SINGING   July 2009

Oh, that darn Blackbird! It's been singing all day. As the urge takes me I join in. I can whistle a bit – lick my lips, curl my tongue into what I hope is the optimum shape for sound quality and project a few musical phrases towards him – to which he replies, right back, copying my crude notes and adding cadences of his own. Then I whistle a few back and he answers again, but oh so beautifully, professional and perfect with his humanly-impossible-to-reproduce tones, undertones, counter-tones, overtones, chucklings and chortlings, burblings and bell-tinklings. I venture a few more notes back, to which he replies again, challenging me with a liquid 'follow this if you dare' golden stream of sound.

ANOTHER STORY

Then rounding off with a touch of mischief, his final notes burst on the air like they'd been forcibly expelled from a rusty, old tin-can.

But he doesn't mind me at all. Seems in fact to be enjoying this game of back and forth. Even though my efforts are pretty pathetic I'm enjoying it too. Not caring that I'm a poor partner. I wonder if he sees me as a monster-sized chick? As night comes on he's still there perched at the top of a bare branch patiently coaching me in the arts of song.

Kuthumi: *He sees you as a wonderful playmate.... He plays with you as he feels the beauty in your music.....*

e-mail of August 8th '09

Dearest Kuthumi,

This summer, except for one week at the beginning of July, has been AWFUL – dark, cold and wet, wet, wet. My blackbird stopped singing, and of course I put it down to the non-stop rain, although it's well known that song birds go quiet around mid-summer. But just recently I noticed that he and his missis have set up home again, built a nest and are hatching a second brood. In the meantime a black cat has adopted us. It's very affectionate, and affection-seeking, but not the least house-trained. Then we heard from a neighbour that it had been brought down from the wilds of Scotland where it lived by hunting. Now in its new home the owners allow it its untamed free range which it exploits by killing lots of birds – including a rare pair of nuthatches which were nesting in our friend's garden.

Next thing is I see the black cat getting extremely interested in the bush in our garden where the blackbirds are nesting– the chicks are now hatched and making a lot of noise when they feel hungry and Mr and Mrs Blackbird fly to and fro working their socks off trying to keep up with them. As the days pass the black feral cat becomes a menace, scrambling into the bush all teeth and claws.

I don't want to injure her by chucking pebbles at her, so fill a squeezy bottle with water ready to give her a shock enough to send her off. I can't have my eyes on her all day, so I'm inside the house working when I hear a great commotion– blackbird's alarm call. One brown and one black Blackbird swooping and alarm-calling as they wing and curve from side to side across the garden. I rush out, but the cat scarpers.

Next day there's a break in the clouds and a glimpse of sun; I thank the gods and grab my coffee to drink outside. The cat appears, purring, winding round my feet, wanting to make friends again. I restrain myself from stroking her because I know her history now. Undeterred, she stretches out her back against the warm flagstones pawing the air – and the occasional butterfly. As much as I'd enjoy relaxing as much as she seems to be doing in this moment of unaccustomed warmth, I know I can't: I'm watching her. Soundlessly, when she thinks I've lost interest, she moves away and starts creeping up the garden path towards the bush. I follow her, all the while speaking severely. I tell her, DO NOT EVEN THINK IT. She throws me a defiant look and continues her steady evil progress to the bush.

I run back to the house and snatch the bottle of water, turn and speed up the path just as she reaches for the nest. I take aim and swash her with a jet of water. Two things happen simultaneously: as the water shoots out of the bottle, the male blackbird darts from the bush, his wings wide like a Tornado plane. He swoops, dives and clips the cat on her head at the exact instant the water hits her! The cat squawks, drops to the ground and hares off down the path pursued by self and blackbird.

The cat, way ahead of me, crouches for take off and leaps over the gate into next-door's garden. As she does my blackbird attacks again, wings outspread and on target for her head he strikes another glancing blow. The cat, mid-air, over its shoulder shoots me a look of uncomprehending horror. A blackbird getting the better of a flying cat is an experience neither of us has witnessed before.

Five minutes later, the cat nowhere to be seen now, all is peace and quiet. Less than a yard from where I'm standing the blackbird settles on a bare branch, cocks his head and looks me right in the eye. I look back and smile. Quietly he begins to sing. I hardly dare believe it. I smile at him and he nods and looks back again, eye to eye. He sings again, sweetly and gently. I acknowledge this in my usual way; I whistle back; he listens, then sings again. I answer this with another whistled tune. Then I walk back slowly and go into the house to carry on with my work.

We haven't seen the cat again for over a week.

'Wow......' said Kuthumi, *'your blackbird is showing you things unimaginable... seems you are teaching him while he teaches you. You have shown him that it is his right to declare his space....and he showed you that he can take care of himself. The cat...well the cat has learned that power does not always serve you in the way you knew it could. Your friendship will continue...*

This is also a timely reminder to honour others choices....there will be birds that won't get away from the cat....and you are not responsible for them. It is no accident that your blackbird has chosen the energy of your backyard.'

DREAMING WORLDS AWAKE

FRAGMENTS ON THE WIND
A SCATTER OF POEMS

FRAGMENTS ON THE WIND

I needed to breathe. Cooped up and corralled by stale thoughts,
I set out. Strode into the gale – set sail, you could have said,
as I had to thrust my hands tight into pockets – so strong it was,
the wind, flapping at the wings of my unfastened summer-light
coat, it would tear it from my body.

So I sallied through viridian fields past amber clad beech
– having crossed the road – sailing in a multi-spacial convoy
of off-white, off-black clouds; I, across green earth, while they,
scudding and racing, plied their blue ethereal oceans. And in that
space between, a flurry of sunlit copper leaves.

Overhead trees bending now to the gale, I shoved through briar
and saw-edged grass to join an unknown path. Snapped twigs
and spent husk pattered on my head along with burnt paper
and flying soot. One piece – like a fragment of chimney's
inner skin it was, layered, built up over time, so it had more
body to it – it lay there at my foot.

Jet intense and fragile, it would have smashed but I stood:
stooped with thumb and finger poised, assessing its size and weight.
Watching how the wind teased and tugged, I saw it tremble, yet, clinging
with such tenacity it gripped its ground; held on with steel-like claws.
Then, minute and berry-red, I saw a pair of hands spread out beside its
pointed snout, and behind, a pair of scuttling feet disappearing into brush.

Sept 2009

FRAGMENTS ON THE WIND

AFTER A STORM

My head turning to the late October sun,
our faces exchange smiles. An old felled tree
shares its warmth as my legs rest their weight.
Nothing visible moves: not a blade; not a leaf.
Dull thud of boot on leather the only sound;
a distant shout, a bark from a faraway field,
while round me the still grass gleams
green like spears and shards of glass.

Oct. 2009

SPEAKING OF SILENCE

Speaking of silence — I cannot.
My eyes close on a breath,
and a blackbird flies in at one ear
and a chaffinch at the other.
I feel the glistening kiss of buttercups
brush my feet. My eyelids part
and a daisy loves me; loves me not.

Oct. 2009

SHE

Words fall short.
Stars slip slantwise
from dark streams.
You live in me, dance through my blood;
a beat, a pulse behind my ear, your
whisper. Moon's small slender fingers
reach into my heart.
Stars fall.
Words drop away.

Late August, 2009

DREAMING WORLDS AWAKE

ANOTHER JOHN : ANOTHER SHAMAN?

This John, Professor John Skeaping, Head of the School of Sculpture at the Royal College while I was a student there in the late 50s was, it now seems to me, also a Shaman – although the term was unknown to me back then. He ran his department – loosely – loosely speaking, by being absent most of the time. Although his influence and 'presence' was much in evidence. He believed – as do many, including myself – that art can't be taught. You can teach craftsmanship, but not art. This hands-not-on approach of his, or excuse for frequent absence was, that the college provided us with everything we needed, and it was up to us to take from the pot of plenty what would most serve us. As adults, we must now learn to teach ourselves by working hard and selecting from all that was on offer; free materials, grand studios, life models of all shapes, genders and dispositions, (including once a white thoroughbred stallion who had starred, along with Laurence Olivier, in one of the most acclaimed movies of the day, *Henry the Fifth*). All of this, plus an assortment of tutors and technical assistants with their designated aside-rooms set about with a plethora of equipment, water tanks, oxy-acetylene welding cylinders, and a gas ring for coffee breaks which doubled as source of heat for bending metal and creating red-hot chisels, was at our disposal. Also at our disposal, was a king-sized bath in the ladies' toilet room with masses of hot water. What more could any student wish for?

ANOTHER JOHN : ANOTHER SHAMAN?

– especially if that left John free to nip over to Ireland and place a bob or three on the horses every now and then.

I put the word 'presence' in quotes because it had a particular meaning for John. He told us that in the horse-dealing world, of which he undoubtedly knew a thing or two, that when picking a good colt or filly for his stable, a racehorse owner would finally make his choice by getting a sense of the animal's 'presence': or he'd decide whether in fact the beast actually had this peculiar quality after all. This ability to sniff out presence was something – an undefinable knack, call it – which you either had or hadn't. John, apparently had it. He also used this 'nose' of his when getting a feel for students – which of them would finally make it – come out winners, which in this case meant being given a much sought-after place at this college. Others, the panel of tutors at our interview for instance, would indulge in long-drawn out interrogations, interview techniques which asked searching questions as to our background, range of interests and experience, while John would loll back – until he suddenly got the sniff, and then select.

When he did put in an appearance, (and it was seldom to make comments on our work), his own 'presence' had a kind of aura which inspired and uplifted. As if drawn by a peculiar magnetism a small group would gather around him in the hope he would tell us another of his tales drawn from his own experience. Before his appointment to the college he had written a book based on his journey to Mexico in 1949. On the face of it the trip was a perverse decision. He'd been very ill at the time and nowhere near recovered from a serious operation. His doctors told him he must slow down, quit alcohol and cigs, confine himself to a diet of easily digestible foods – mashed potato, milk and fish. If not he could exacerbate his condition and the consequences of *that*... They wouldn't be held responsible... Ignoring the advice he told himself: 'If they think I'm about to pop my clogs, I'll take the trip anyway. Better to live life to the full and risk the consequences, than spend my life on pobs.' Whether the fact that a Mexican villager's diet might include bloody red meat sold from roadside markets buzzing with flies, lashings of beans and high doses of chilli at every meal was in his mind when he made this decision, he didn't say, but I guess it must have been.

I managed to track down a second-hand copy of his book only recently; until then I hadn't read it. It's full of riveting stories of his time out there, but the one thing I'd looked for but didn't find was the experience which caused me to see him as a shaman. It was from various other incidents which he'd recounted during our period as students, one in particular of a visitation, that this idea began to gel. He'd been married to the sculptress Barbara Hepworth and they had a son, Paul. Early in the War Paul was called up – or joined of his own free will – and was serving in the Royal Air Force. One night John awoke, startled to find the boy sitting at the foot of the bed. Impossible! He knew his son was miles away, the other side of the world. He'd had a phone call from him only days ago. 'Can't give you any details, dad. We're not allowed, but we're due to go on some kind of mission in a day or two. Ring you when we get back safe,' his son had said. Yet here he was in the bedroom!

'What are you doing here!' John whispered. Now he wasn't sure if he was in the grip of a dream or an hallucination.

'It's OK dad,' the boy said. 'Don't be scared, but I wanted to let you know this way so you can tell mum before she gets the telegram. It'll be with you in a few days, but if you can tell her first it will be less of a shock. We crashed. I'm alright though.'

'Alright?' John asked, his voice weak with hope, tremulous from emotion.

ANOTHER JOHN : ANOTHER SHAMAN?

'I'm in a different place now dad. I shan't be coming back, not back home to earth, but I'm OK. It's a good place here where I am. Have to go now though.' With that the image of his son faded and disappeared.

'The condolence telegram arrived in due course.' That statement John delivered matter-of-fact. We sat silent, all kinds of questions starting in our minds, but all seemed stupid or banal in the face of what we'd just heard. Someone did begin to enquire how many days it took for the telegram... but let his words hang in the air. No-one voiced disbelief or asked, how did his mother take it. Did she even *believe* you? Continuing matter-of-fact, John wondered in his usual tone if we weren't ready to get back to work yet. We drifted off to our respective studios still with our unspoken thoughts.

On another occasion he entertained us with a 'hot from the press' incident. The previous day he'd taken Princess Margaret out in his Rolls Royce for lunch at the Dorchester – I think that was it – or maybe the Savoy. However, they'd been turned away at the door. Not only was John without a tie – that could be fixed – the doorman would discretely lend him the appropriate item which he kept secreted in his locker especially for these embarrassing contingencies. However, what could not be tolerated was that John had committed the unforgivable sin: he'd drawn up to the grand portals in a re-sprayed Roller of two-tone cream and green.

These impromptu chats where John let us into his life, interspersed with bouts of concentrated creation, were intrinsic elements of the full-of-surprises, capricious wind which blew through the corridors of our sculpture school. Well known figures from the contemporary art scene dropping in were normal; Henry Moore, Jacob Epstein, notable architects and distinguished art critics of the day each in their distinctive apparel. Feelings around the sort of stir caused by the appearance of the odd Star of Stage or Screen fishing for a portrait on the cheap, were more ambivalent. Though the stir when a famous model or current mistress of the great Epstein dropped in was far more appreciative.

Once, a strikingly good looking female arm-in-arm with Jacob stopped me in the corridor. 'Jacob, look!' she said. 'Here's that girl I told you about. I think she'll make a good subject for a head, don't you?' Jacob moved closer and placed a gnarled and muscular finger under my chin. I froze. He turned my head from side to side and a'hummed thoughtfully. Then they walked on allowing my awe-struck paralysis to unfreeze slightly and, lest it turn to a puddle, I rushed away for a strong coffee.

Epstein was 'in residence' around that time. He'd been given a commission for a colossal sculpture, probably the largest piece of work anyone had attempted since the ancients of Egypt, Greece or Rome – though if you count the Statue of Liberty as sculpture... But certainly the largest figure I've personally seen. This commission, rumour had it, was for a figure of The Risen Christ, and it was to be cast into bronze. But that required a preliminary model in clay from which a plaster mould would next be taken before handing over to the London bronze foundry. Epstein, at this time, lived a short walk away close by Kensington Gore. His studio, spacious enough for most of his civic commissions up to now, was far too small for this monster work. He'd sought out Skeaping on the possibility of using one of ours, the largest belonging to Skeaping himself. The deal had been arranged and Jacob became a regular sight of a morning, eager to start his day's work along with the rest of us. Except that his eagerness was a good deal more apparent than ours.

Lingering outside around the doorway in the sunshine with mugs of coffee, or squatting on blocks of carving stone stubbing butt ends into planting troughs, we plotted how we could best sneak up Queensgate and across Ken High to the Serpentine in Hyde Park for a swim. 'Moin'n, bwoys and goyls,' the now-familiar grizzly bear-man growled as he passed us, traces of Bronx accent, in his exuberance, breaking through. And beaming beatifically he'd head in at the door, with a, 'Great day f'woik.'

His 'woik' progressed steadily. Curiosity burning, I took a peep into the master studio now and then. A pair of feet were slowly creeping across the floor – clay feet, in my estimation a good five meters, or if you prefer, 15ft of feet, long! Next time I looked – I'd been invited on the pretext of helping our materials technician to unload a few more bags of clay onto the studio floor – the feet had sprouted a pair of ankles, calves and knees. Next time, a massive trunk seemed to have materialised overnight. Jacob must have felt particularly inspired by the weather that week and been 'woik'n' overtime. By the time an impressive head began its ascent, eyes fixed upon the glass ceiling high above, we had a pair of giant legs in one corner, an equally gigantic lower torso in the centre of the room, and a magnificent chest, shoulders, neck and head in the other corner. The poem Ozymandias by Shelley leapt to mind: *I met a traveller from an antique land who said: Two vast and trunkless legs of stone stand in the desert... Near them on the sand, half sunk, a shattered visage lies, whose frown and wrinkled lip, and sneer of cold command tell that its sculptor well those passions read...* The 'visage' before us on the ground lacked any such negative passions: this Christ figure's expression was that of a gloriously transcendent triumph over death. I remember us all standing around at this point marvelling, but wondering if the sections would join up, and how on earth could this present-day master sculptor have calculated each stage of the process so well that the proportions might be an exact and perfect fit. All it required now was to get it all out of the door and off to wherever it was destined to go for the rest of the process; casting and piecing it all together. But I digress....

Skeaping as Shaman. And that Big Tree of Mexico. But the story I was looking for wasn't in that book, not as I remember it being told to us. I read it through, enjoying it; intrigued and fascinated to have this insight into John the setting-out sculptor meeting and later living among Mexican villagers who had no word for art or artist, yet painted, sculpted and potted enduring masterpieces. As students he'd recounted at another of his informal chats how he came to be appointed Spiritual Godfather, or *Padrino* to a family of indigenous Indians. This was a great honour, one which conferred not only kudos, but also a few unforeseen responsibilities. It was the first time in living memory such a role had been bestowed on a white man, never mind one recently arrived from over the great waters. But now, as an integrated member of this community – I think 'Compadre' had been added to his title – just as he'd been accepted by them, he adapted himself to their way of life. Sharing one's good fortune with others who found themselves suddenly in need, was taken for granted. So, when members of 'his' family succumbed one by one to an unidentifiable disease, without a second's thought John's instinct was to provide for them as best he could. Sadly, as the weeks passed, several of the youngest and frailer oldest died. Learning the ways of a good neighbour was one thing, but beyond that, certain spiritual powers were attributed to the Padrone. John discovered it was also up to him to preside over some very unfamiliar and bizarre funeral rites, Catholic and pre-Christian Zapotec. Superstition and the supernatural blurred into religion.

Even more onerous was the spiritual responsibility laid upon him due to the strange belief that if the Padrone was

ANOTHER JOHN : ANOTHER SHAMAN?

absent from the village and the ahijado or Godchild died, then the fault would be his: his absence the cause of the death. The other side of that coin – when another young girl, this time John's *ahijada*, (or God-daughter) lying at death's door, made a remarkable recovery, that was attributed to John's miraculous healing powers. The fact that he'd driven, tense with apprehension, through the previous night to a reputable doctor a hundred miles away to obtain the latest Western medicines was dismissed, in an interesting reversal of Western beliefs, as superficial coincidence.

The epidemic had by then been diagnosed as typhoid: the village well, its source. Luckily John had been vaccinated before leaving England, but the water continued to be drunk and the vulnerable continued to die. He'd gone on to tell us – whether then or some other story-telling session, I can't remember – that during this outbreak another close friend, a woman from the village, had lost her baby son. Wearily, she'd walked some distance to tell him, and broken down in tears as her story poured out. Drawing herself together with dignity she'd overcome her grief and gone on to ask him a favour. Her husband was away – she didn't know how to contact him – yet because of the epidemic the boy had to be buried next day. Would John accompany her and another friend – there was no other way – John's was the only car and they had to find the child's father – bring him back, or the funeral rites would be incomplete and the little one refused entry to Angel's paradise.

John agreed readily but not without some trepidation. His old banger was barely roadworthy and the father was at least a hundred and fifty miles away. It was almost dark when they set off with only the vaguest idea of where, in the vast wild countryside, this man might be. The friend accompanying them, let's call him Pablo, had this feeling in his bones that if they drove in a certain direction into the mountains his 'senses' would probably pick up clues on the way. He was sure, he said, crossing himself vigorously as they wound up the steep and precarious track through the foothills, that with John present the Eternal Father would be with them too. Struggling with the steering, John followed suit, crossing himself. Neither he nor this vehicle on its wobbly old wheels with its spluttering and coughing old engine was likely make it without Divine assistance.

They'd made it into the mountains now, and there'd been a brief and awesome twilight for a few moments; then pitch-black. The exhausted woman seemed to have fallen asleep in the back. Dark peaks loomed ominously over the narrowest of tracks when Pablo abruptly hissed, 'Stop!' Applying the brakes suddenly would have been fatal, but John slowed to a halt as soon as he safely could. 'What? Why?' John asked.

'Don't know,' came the whispered reply, 'but get out with me now.'

As they scrambled out into the blackness, Pablo murmured, 'Shhh. What do you hear?'

No danger of any other vehicle rushing at them up here; nothing to be heard but absolute silence. 'Nothing. I don't hear a thing,' John told him.

Pablo took a few steps forward and beckoned. They stood gazing into the night. 'What do you see? Up there,' Pablo gestured toward the peaks.

'Still nothing,' whispered John, puzzled.

Pablo turned back to the car. 'OK. On a bit further then.'

The engine was coaxed into life once more and the journey resumed. John peering at the road and Pablo into the hills, they crawled on until his companion lifted his hand in a signal. 'Here!'

'What? Out again?' John asked.

ANOTHER JOHN : ANOTHER SHAMAN?

Pablo nodded. 'What do you see now? Up there?'

John's eyes gradually adjusting to the conditions, he scanned an undulating horizon riven with clefts and gulleys. Ash grey and charcoal scrub came into focus, sentinel cactus shapes, ink black depths which might have been caves. Then, something! 'What's that? he hissed. 'I think I can see a fire.'

Pablo slapped him on the shoulder, 'Yes!' he yelled. 'That's him.'

And so it proved to be.

The journey back with the father proved even more hazardous. First one tyre burst, then a wheel came off, lastly the engine packed up entirely. We never found out how it all ended; it was time for us to get back to work again before the story finished its course, though not before John managed to give us Pablo's parting remark: 'As I told you, Compadre. None of this would have been accomplished without you. Indeed, the Eternal Father was with you.'

* * *

Maybe the evidence for putting John Skeaping forward as a candidate for Shaman is a bit thin. Certainly nothing of that sort occurred to me while I was a student, nor in the subsequent decades. Only from this point, today, looking back fifty years, can I see threads joining up. In 1949, the year John went to Mexico, I must have been about fourteen and in my third year in Junior Art School with any thought of ending up in a London college so distant it hadn't crossed my mind. Also absent from my mind was the fact that I'd once been given a little book from the series, 'How to Draw...' as a birthday present from an uncle: I'd forgotten. Yet many years later when I spotted it hiding between much larger volumes on my shelf, opening it I realised just what an impact it must have had on me as a child. Across the pages of this *How to Draw Horses* by John Skeaping galloped, reared, stamped and

DREAMING WORLDS AWAKE

whinnied a stream of free-flowing charcoal, pen and ink equestrian images – quick strokes capturing with an accuracy only a man who knew his subject from the inside could achieve. Spontaneous, impressionistic, they came to life on the paper. Often, typically, he'd used his fingers, smudging charcoal, and, dipped in ink, dappling the flanks of piebald yearlings. How different this children's drawing book was from most of the others, whether childish cartoons or careful academic studies, of its time.

If this forgotten book was where my contact with his spirit began, it continued long after. I never knew when the flesh and blood, already in his seventies, man I'd met in his role of Professor of the School of Sculpture, died. Life had moved on for me – taken many unexpected turns. Any recollection I may have had of John's prediction that morning when we nervously gathered around him for his parting words, was shoved away with a lot of other inconvenient stuff. Convocation had been only days away – the great Day when, in ludicrous caps and gowns we would take our place on the platform waiting to be led by our respective Heads of School to receive our scrolls at the hand of Robin Darwin, our Principle. John spoke to us in turn that morning – how he'd watched our progress over the past three years – how he'd argued each case with Darwin – told him how he knew more intimately our potential than was superficially apparent in the work we'd displayed in our final exhibition. He turned to me. To say I was uncomfortable is an understatement; I'd already seen my dismal results on the notice board.

'We all thought you had promise' he told me. 'At your interview we were agreed – you had more about you than some of the others, yet right now it seems that promise hasn't been fulfilled. Which doesn't meant it won't be in the future, but you need more time – and more experience. You need

61

time to experiment and explore, and that might mean you'll discover other ways to express yourself. You don't have to stick with sculpture even – you may become a writer. But whatever you do decide for the future, one thing I've always been certain of: You're an artist; you have 'presence.'

* * *

About ten years ago when Michael and I were doing another bit of household clearing out, he brought me a copy of ARC, the student's journal of the Royal College of Art. He'd found it in the attic and though he'd better ask me if I wanted to keep it. I started to look it through, memories flying out as I flipped through the pages. 'Keep it, I said.

The following day, Kirsten, my friend, rang the doorbell. She seemed breathless. Told me she'd just arrived back in Bath and come straight here before going to her own house. 'No I won't come in', she said. 'Must get back home, but I had to see you first.'

'Where's the fire? Why're you in such a tearing hurry?'

'I've just been down to Devon – this old school reunion.'

I waited, shrugging my shoulders. Still couldn't see the fuss.

'I met someone – one of the people from my old school – someone I never got on with. He used to be so rude, gave me a bad time at school when I was this outsider, vulnerable, just joining long after the term began. They'd all ganged up and rejected me. Well, he came up to me just now and actually apologised for the past. Invited me back to his home in Devon. He lives there now. Right there on the coffee table with a lot of other stuff was this magazine – a really old copy – an ARC. I told him I thought you'd been there, and perhaps knew his father.'

'His father?' I still didn't get it.

'Didn't I tell you?' she said, still breathless. 'His name is Skeaping; John Skeaping's son[*]. I wasn't sure of my facts,' she went on, 'but there was something about that ARC. It actually had an article by his father inside about some student – Sydney Harpley. (Yes, the very Syd Harpley that appeared in the Dido/Momo dream.) We talked about it, and I said I thought you knew him – his father, that is. Weren't you one of his students? Anyhow, there was something about that cover, the way it looked at me from the table. I felt I just had to come and ask if it meant anything to you.'

Every front cover of ARC was unique; different designs by current students over the years. But she then went on to describe the one she'd seen. I shivered and my mouth went dry. It was the same one which Michael had brought me only the day before.

* This incidentally was Skeaping's son by another marriage.

SYNCHRONICITY
= Topping the Charts
(Oct. 17th 2009)

Oh, here we go, I thought, Synchronicity strikes again, as hardly had I finished recalling my all-too-brief encounter with Jacob Epstein in the last chapter, when I heard the contemporary, Angel of the North sculptor, Anthony Gormley, broadcasting a tribute to him – a prelude to a major exhibition opening at the Royal Academy to commemorate his death 50 years ago. One of the giants, and solely responsible for the arrival of modernism in this country, Gormley said of him. On the very same day I caught another piece of news: Carl Jung was in the *top three best sellers* list at Amazon. Both men had for decades been decidedly out of fashion. Both, however, regarded by myself as major figures with something important to say – more so now than ever.

* * *

Epstein was possibly the most innovative major sculptor to hit Britain at the beginning of the last century, and his presence had certainly left its mark on me. Yet, in those few years while I was at college in London another revolution in the world of the plastic arts was under way. Painting and sculpture were thrown back into the crucible as new, grand-scale works flooded in from the States. Once again 'the public' were outraged. The press of course love a spot of outrage and the public never tire of obliging them with copy. In previous centuries first Constable and Turner incensed them with their impressionistic 'smears,' then James MacNeill Whistler's infamous 'Black and Gold: The Falling Rocket' with its breathtaking firework display of paint on canvas. During the libel case which Whistler had brought against him, the art critic Ruskin accused him of impudence and ill-educated conceit for asking the public 200 guineas to have a pot of paint flung in their faces. And now in the second half of the fifties here was the painter Jackson Pollock inviting another wave of hostility by dribbling paint all over his canvases and daring to call that art.

While painters swept convention aside with wild abandoned tar-brush strokes, like that other Abstract Expressionist, Franz Kline or, more appalling still, rode bicycles, tyres coated with house-paint, over canvas sheets, sculptors too rode their imaginations down strange new highways. Until then they'd been content with natural and organic stone, metal or wood as their medium of expression, but now man-made materials were about to be explored and the latest techniques exploited. Within ten years of my leaving college work which had so shocked the public at the first half of the century was suddenly out-dated, and soon to be ignored. Epstein was 'out', abstract carving 'old hat', as purple, green, and pink fibreglass made its bid for attention. Multi-coloured plastics slithered snake-like across gallery floors and public spaces, or reared gaudy pennants in an angular two-fingered salute to the traditionalist art lover.

Wrestling with what it means to be a creator I am drawn back to my twenty-something student self and the struggle I had trying to make sense of the maelstrom which swirled around me – a confusion of possibilities and choices. Yet I'm back again in that crucible – feeling part of it, yet apart from it at the same time. Fifty years on, older but hopefully wiser, although some elements seem familiar, I'm free from my earlier bewilderment. The myriad potentials on offer here today were undreamed of then. Avenues have opened up within me which allow me to move beyond the limited, time-bound, three-dimensional world I once inhabited. Now, along with any other human who chooses, I can play in an expanded universe of my own creating, one which encompasses not only past and future, but allows another kind of going back.

This is new. Really new. It works with a new kind of energy requiring a new kind of consciousness. This 'going back' is different, for instance, from how, with the benefit of our present-day psychological insights, we are able to re-experience and transmute past mistakes or abusive experiences, essential as this might be. From this new perspective we can open portals which, although they may have existed before, in what we *call* the past, were invisible, lying unconsciously in some other part of ourselves.

> Yes, said Kuthumi, *this is about simply acknowledging that potentials that may not have been chosen in that moment are still viable and possible. It is about letting go of the linearity of how you see your choices play out. That A leads to B and then C and then D.....because sometimes even though you are at the D from one choice of pathway, the D (or even W) of the path of another choice can still intersect with your present!*

This is a freedom of choice far exceeding anything our present culture, even at the cutting edge of science or philosophy, accepts as real or possible. Our artists have been doing this work for us over the years, breaking down barriers, flinging paint in our faces, while we, 'the public,' are in turns aghast, envious, or down-right confounded and bamboozled. What to make of you, the artist in society? (You see I include myself in both categories now.) Are we being taken for a ride by you? 'My child can do better than that,' we said of Picasso's scrawls. And Picasso replied, 'Oh, that you *were* that child.' 'When I was twelve years old I drew like Raphael,' he said. 'It's taken me the rest of my life to learn to draw like a child.'

DREAMING WORLDS AWAKE

We imagine the world moves forward; science and technology, art and philosophy progress in a linear fashion. Or do they? Maybe Art is the exception, maybe it has more tricks up its sleeve. Back in the cauldron again; give it a stir and see what comes bubbling up to the surface. Cauldron: crucible: what matter! same difference! *And a little child shall lead them.*

* * *

Born in East Side New York to Polish Jewish emigrants circa 1880, Epstein the artist was the target of vilification and ridicule for much of his adult life. His 1927 Strand carvings in London, for instance, were attacked both verbally and physically smashed. Others were bought by a businessman and displayed in a freak show at Blackpool. Now, October 2009, as I write, we have this commemoration exhibition. Fifty years dead. And I myself, fifty or so years on, begin to see him in a new light. He lives again! But what will the public reaction be this time I wonder? Hopefully they'll see something more significant this time round.

I'd always admired him and his work greatly, but there were a few carvings which, in my twenties, I'd never been too comfortable with. I was aware that when he'd first shown them to the public around 1900 to 1930, there had been an uproar, people calling them obscene, brutish, ugly. My reactions as a student in the second half of the 1950s didn't go anywhere near that far, but I had found these figures disturbing. Yet now it seems I'm being drawn towards them, and deeper into them – drawn back *by* them into my own origins, and into a deeper connection with the meaning of Creatorship.

Where better to start than with Epstein's carving of *Adam*, the First Man, Ancestor of us all.

SYNCHRONICITY – Topping the Charts

ADAM

In the clutter of the sculptor's studio... going back... a block of alabaster standing in the corner. It's been there for some time, several years. I remember rescuing it from that workshop... knowing I would work with it some day. The men were about to slice it into slabs – veneers – for whatever had been ordered by their customers; counter tops, shop-front facings, floors for smart hotels, but I felt sadness for it as it stood there about to be butchered. It was too noble a thing to be sacrificed in that way. So I handed over my good money and it was mine. It's been waiting patiently here in my studio ever since... patient, just as myself, patient, waiting for it to speak.

It often invites me to touch it, like now ... beckoning me to it. I'm making my way between stands smeared with clay – plaster spattered plinths – a ladder against the wall. I push carefully past a part-finished nude and between a crowd of portrait heads; vital and rosy-cheeked children, one pale and sick, quietly looking inward. Women wearing the many faces of Eve, their strong beauty radiating from an inner grace, rather than cosmetically altered glamour. They stand flanked by a rank of exalted dignitaries; the poet Tagore, Nehru, Emperor Haile Salasie, Einstein. No worldly powerful women there, you'll notice: their time hasn't yet come. I wonder what I'd have made of the Mesdames Meier, Gandhi, Sirimavo Bandaranyeke, or indeed Madam Thatcher, if they'd presented themselves to me? As I move on there's a sensation like an icy finger pricking up the hair at the back of my neck. I'm being scrutinised by these presences, departed and not yet arrived. Ahh! the block, my alabaster, we're face to face, again each observing the other. I run my hand down its surface, lightly dusting it, smelling, caressing it. And I pause ... what is it? A frisson, a sense beneath my hand of a slight tremor as the alabaster grows warm and a tracery of iron veins pulses through its pale calcite body. A connection fires in my fingertips... telegraph wires hum with strange intimations travelling across an immensity of time and distance. I smile: my alabaster block is speaking to me at last.

In the sedimentary depths of a lake – an ocean – a million million tiny bones and shells float by and settle, layer upon layer, building, sinking, forming, while a weight of water presses down. Life swarms, feasts and dies, discards its carapace. Creeping out from the primal soup something new struggles onto land, grasping at it with rudimentary stubs for limbs that will, in time, stride forth to lord the Earth.

Yet embedded still in an infinity of time, never moving, this layer of calciferous rock, patient, ever patient, lies. I can be patient too: I've waited many years for it to begin its story, yet the swirl of my life continues. Creation goes on. There's work to attend to, and I make to move away as I have many times before. But my hand lingers. Another signal has arrested me. Gaia yawns and stretches, Earth cracks open, shockwaves explode, great continental shelves are shifting. The World wakes from its Dream.

Thus sayeth the Lord: 'I will shake: The heavens and the earth, the sea and the dry land, I will shake, and every valley shall be exalted, every mountain and hill made low,' *thus spake I AM.*

Where there had been silent and immovable depths, now, towering, rippling and bending walls of rock reach up to the skies before crashing down again. The Earth is on the move, recreating herself; calciferous bedrock metamorphosing, becoming alabaster.

High up on the ceiling of the Pope's chapel Michelangelo balances astride the scaffolding. His mind, like that of the poet Yeats, moves upon silence, and, brush in hand, he adds a final touch. God reaches out, and across the gap between His and Adam's finger the spark leaps again. Michelangelo steadies himself, sweating. The shock's almost knocked him off his perch!

Our Jacob's sweaty too, but I see he's picked up his chisels, fingering the points and claws, wondering which of them to use for the first roughing out of his block.

And so it was, and so it is: Jacob's *Adam* comes into being.

The group of carvings which caused so much public outrage in Nineteen-thirty nine, and even for me, some difficulty, included this 'Adam'. It was a powerful piece with a strongly primitive face, and, because it had been carved from a single block of alabaster which he happened to have in his studio, its proportions were somewhat squat. Many voices were

E.E

raised against this depiction of the First Man, Ancestor of the human race, saying it had represented him in a grossly unflattering light. Epstein himself said of it that although he had a fairly clear idea when he'd conceived it, as it progressed it developed a law of its own. In spite of the restriction the block imposed, he'd managed to get a tremendous movement within it, a movement springing, not from flung out forms, but from an inner energy – like a dynamo.

This freedom of expression that Epstein was not afraid to bring into reality is the freedom of creativity that ALL man seeks. It is about being brave enough to express it. Thank the heavens that people like him exist to push boundaries and open up perceptions. Yes sometimes it begins as re-hashing or combining influences but this is all part of the creative process. As you know in Egypt art did not change in any significant way for thousands of years. So take time to thank yourself, Esmé, for being made to feel uncomfortable by his work... how wonderful that you allowed yourself that choice!

Bravery in creativity is the key to expansion. It is one thing to be brave enough to make art that the world may scorn but that is nothing compared to wanting to make a sculpture or painting and then submitting to self doubt. For every Adam sculpture there are millions of creations that have never made their way beyond the imagination of the artist. This reflection is your reminder to push your boundaries, to create with no expectations from yourself or anyone else! said Kuthumi.

THE ROCK DRILL

But the one work above all which disturbed and enraged the populace had been created some twenty years earlier around the beginning of the First World War. Although it was probably conceived before that – conceived and dreamed into being. This dream however was rather more of a nightmarish vision of Things To Come. If Jacob's telephone wires had buzzed with messages from the far off origins of Mankind as his *Adam* drew slowly into being, they had earlier transmitted a terrifying vibration from the Future – the sound of boots goose-stepping down the streets of Paris, Rome and Berlin. A machine was on the march – a War Machine. No longer would men stand face to face with drawn swords or rifles, the grotesque image of Mechanised Man; Warrior devoid of eyes or heart or soul was about to roll forth.

Did I dream it? I don't know. What I do know is I threw myself into the excitement. Paris in those years before the First World War was the hub of activity for those who saw themselves as revolutionaries – artists of all kinds; composers, dancers, poets, writers, even the philosophers – you name it. Revolution was in the air and I went headlong into it. I'd sought it, been drawn there, and there it was conceived. My Rock Drill. My contribution to the movement – or the plethora of movements of the time; futurists, pre-fascists, modernists and abstractionists. Ostensibly I was influenced by them, but to tell the truth I soon lost patience with their posings and struttings. How was it that in England they were received with open arms – that is, until the novelty wore off and they retreated back to their homelands to give birth to Mussolini and his ilk? Much of this art was theatrical and superficial – a matchbox tied to a tooth brush, for instance, dangling from a chandelier, while the idiot who'd created it bellowed out his poetry, red in the face, streaming with sweat, veins standing out to busting point on his neck, and all to the accompaniment of another fascist fool beating the hell out of a drum. Exhibitionists trying to shock, and for a time in Paris, I was right in there with them.

Don't mistake me: I saw through their antics, but I was there in the sense that I saw the duty of an artist is to overthrow convention. This I saw as a sleep, a soporific drift that leads to relinquishment of responsibility and all that follows. Sleep: perchance to Dream? There are always those who've sought the sleep of oblivion to dull their pain, but luckily, though I wasn't much aware of this myself, there were other revolutionaries at work. The spirit of the times also begat an enquiry into a subject which had, until then, been the territory of poets, mystics and prophets. Dreams. Set aside the early attempt to formulate symbols and their interpretation, Freud's observation that dreams were the 'Royal Road to the Unconscious' unlocked man's exploration into the human mind and its potential for dreaming new worlds into being.

DREAMING WORLDS AWAKE

Was it a combination of all these elements which led to the emergence of my Rock Drill? Unlike my later pieces which were to attract unwelcome hostility, this was meant to shock from the start. And shock it did: in several ways at once. Yet the question, the same one I'd ask of all art, is: does it stand the test of time? Well, not exactly. This one doesn't stand – because I smashed its legs. Maybe I got cold feet. I was keen to experiment, and for one thing the possibility of introducing mechanics seduced me. I was fascinated by the concept of a man/machine hybrid, and toyed with having its arms linked to pneumatic power, but these ideas were conscious. Child's play. And I dropped them. The thing which both arrested and drove me to the final act of creation was less conscious. As though on some night journey, wandering down a corridor, I'd opened a forbidden door. Foreseen the very form which would epitomise all our worst fears of what the future might bring.

Wrought from metal, ribs like fenders, a bug-browed, raptor-beaked visor for a head, its torso was not so much clad in some protective carapace as worn by knights of old, but no,

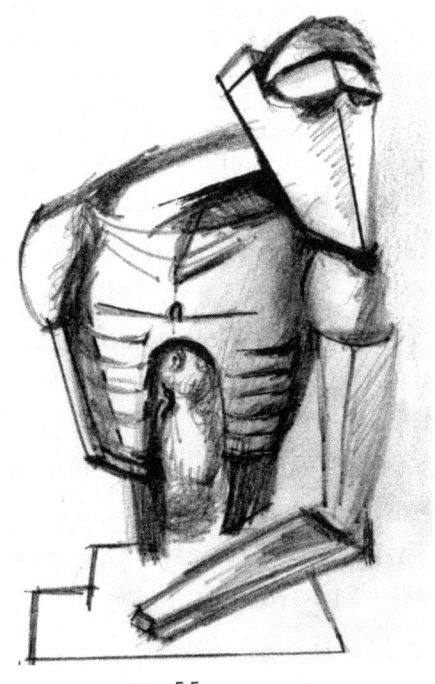

E.E

the body itself was the armour. Erect upon a tripod of steel legs, its iron phallus poised for rape, it became an archetype for alien invasion. Whether conscious or unconsciously other artists, dramatists, film makers, have made use of the image over and again, though it was I who'd gazed into the abyss and drawn it forth. Machines for mass destruction I realised would enable mankind to kill from a safe distance without the inconvenience of blood on their hands or the screams of slaughtered flesh on their consciences.

Embodied in its metal breast, below where its heart should have been, was this foetus – an homunculus of vulnerable flesh. Turning its back on that which lay before it, the view too terrible to face, it has decided never to be born.

JACOB, THE ANGEL AND ME

In the second half of the 1950s Epstein presented us with another work, the shockwaves of which still reverberate to this day: *Jacob and the Angel.* Fused from the waist down, genital organs visible, (though which of the men they belonged to is unclear), the figures are in a life and death embrace. The Angel, with eyes bulging from beneath a jut of brow, stares into the face of the other, his mouth so close, so urgent, it seems about to plant a kiss. His arms grasp Jacob's body, overpowering and at the same time upholding him. As Jacob's head droops backwards his own arms fall away, all energy spent. On the cover of Rushdie's *Satanic Verses* I see another depiction of the same eternal wrestling match. Rushdie asks, 'Can demons be angelic? Can angels be devils in disguise?' And see where that got *him!* Yet, in his three-dimensional depiction of his namesake, Epstein poses a further question. Is it Love which overcomes him? it seems to ask. Are they merging into one – energies combining?

As I see this image now, today, I am struck by its powerful message. Aspects of the human being which are normally, in some parts of the Christian world at any rate, seen as separate, the Divine and the born-in-sin, fallible human, here they're in a process of attaining a Wholeness which embraces both Light and Dark. In *Adam* we were taken back to our origins. With *Rock Drill* we glimpsed a future we now recognise as having materialised to a large extent. These journeys, the geographical, biological highway of life, and the fear driven, power crazed road to destruction, were on a linear time-track: *Jacob and the Angel* dissects the horizontal with a vertical and creates a new dimension. The Self, which exists out of time in the realms of The Divine Now, descends into the physical body of existence. But in a way we least expect! The Dark Angel grasps this son of Adam in the profoundest embrace of love. Some mystery!

* * *

It had to be that, didn't it? Jacob the sculptor struggling with his material, or warring against that tide of scorn and vilification which had threatened to overwhelm him all his life – the outrageous creator sinking beneath a sea of misunderstanding and press-generated bile. Wasn't that what it was all about? Or maybe I was indulging my homo-erotic fantasies. This is certainly what many thought. Or was it, as that voice inside me whispered, the outrageous creator blaspheming against himself, administering the kiss of life and coup de grace *in the same instant? That, and all of the above, I suppose.*

Mastery over material and the limitation it imposes suggests in some paradoxical way that matter both holds and at the same time liberates the spirit – and paradoxically this limitation has been my teacher on my path towards mastery. Once – if I remember it right – a year or two before my death, while I was busy completing my Christ figure in that studio at the Royal College – some student asked why I hadn't become a teacher – like that young Liz Frink, they asked. Only just left college herself apparently, yet been given a post at Chelsea.

I answered without hesitation: Because I haven't done with being a student myself. No criticism of her. I spoke – I almost said, without thinking, but that might be misunderstood too. My response simply came out, no need to consider it. 'But it would be so good to have you here teaching us,' they persisted. I smiled, shrugged and went back to my studio– left them to think it over.

So Esmé, you've had plenty of time by now, to think. How're you doing? Don't gawp like that – I was aware of you. Still am.

There's always the two of you. You and you. Struggling, wrestling. Master and student. And then lightning strikes. A force you'd never expected visits you. A door in some other dark corridor, in someone else's reality, opens, and turns you upside down and inside out. The Greeks strove for the absolutes of proportion and beauty, endowing their gods and goddesses with their ideal of human perfection. Then came the Renaissance a millennium or two later with their Christs and Madonnas; ideals again, but allowing a place for the expression of feeling, factoring in grief and suffering. Their gods were human as well as divine. God made flesh. There was mastery there, but I turned away and looked to Africa and the East – as far as Polynesia – for a new expression which would bring more of our human experience together, striving for wholeness rather than perfection, factoring in the Primitive. Humanity untamed, present in all its rawness and power, sprung naked and unashamed from the source of all life. Adam and Eve before their expulsion from Paradise, wasn't that what you were wrestling with too?

I smiled, watching you unable to 'get it right'. Unable to finish that life-size Adam and Eve model of The Expulsion you were wrestling with in time for your degree show. That degree – what was all that, that scroll of paper which meant so much to you? And our friend Skeaping? Didn't he stumble as he placed his hand on your shoulder, embarrassed as well he might be, participating in that ridiculous charade, all of you like geese in line decked out in caps and gowns. Tripped up did your professor as he touched you. What was that about? Darwin, your principle, grandson himself of the great monkey man, self-important standing there with those twists of paper, and you following in your master's footsteps eager to receive them from the hands of great presence. I smiled again.

Work in progress. Unfinished piece. So, how're we doing now? You don't like the way this is going, huh, this conversation? You thought you'd do a portrait of me, and here am I scrutinising you – again. A portrait, at least one that goes further than reportage, deeper than a copy of what is seen out front, involves two people face to face, sitter and artist; one, in the nakedness of his person enters into a meeting place with the other. An act of co-creation more than skin deep. But how deep, how far shall we dare? What will you allow? Not only head to head, but now a journey of perceptions and instincts where I enter your inner life, and you invite me into the corridors of your interior so that I remake you from the inside out?

And you? What will you make of me in this encounter? Oh, stop! Stop! Where is this going? Is this real, really happening, and how real is real? You ask. Well, student, teacher, master, *am I putting words into your mouth? Are you ready for that meeting which you ducked before? I wouldn't be standing here before you at this moment if you weren't, because this is where you meet your Soul.*

They are afraid of you now, as they were of me, shape-shifter, reality shaper. You already felt the power of the Rock Drill, knew both its dark and light aspects. Rape and Procreation. The phallic penetration of the Matrix, the core of the planet where she rebirths herself – giving birth to New Earth, and man/woman of Divine Genesis takes over from Goddess Gaia. You and you, I and I, co-sculpting a new body, stepping into the shoes of Mastery. Some shoes – some feet. Are you ready? Shall we go further?

Is there further?

Of course.

Oh, my God!

There's your work O sculptor, O shaper of energy, there's all that you have to tell the world about the power to change reality, O wordspinster. It's a big step. Big feat – big step. Let's go. I'll give you A NEW HEADING —

HEADING INTO THE NEW: THE DARK ANGEL

Oh Beloved, you're about to meet your Divinity. Step forth into this new adventure.

This sudden change of tone, coming more like a pronouncement from on high, threw me. It was a different voice, or it seemed so. Who was I speaking to? It didn't sound like – not that I had actually heard Jacob's voice out loud before, but even the interior voice I had been communicating with until now had come with a certain accent and style of speaking which I recognised as the Jacob I had known. 'This doesn't sound like you, Jacob,' I said quietly aloud. 'Or if it is you your voice seems to have changed – stepped up vibrationally. And why do you address me as Beloved, whoever you are?'

'*Shapes shift,*' came the reply. Was that it? Was that all I was to be given? I waited, but still nothing more came. After sitting in growing uncertainty and frustration for quite some time wondering what to do, I decided, maybe I should trust myself to the moment, however unexpected. 'Beloved?' I asked again. 'Why did you address me as beloved?'

You were given this name, Esmé. It means, Beloved, as you know. You were also given the name Mary. You are not only the you you think you are. You are greater than that – much to ponder there. But for another time, maybe, let's move on. When I set those feet on the floor of the studio, my Jacob and the Angel was already behind me – accomplished. It had exploded from some place inside me with an energy which carried me along in its wake. I allowed it to express itself – couldn't stop it, its force was so great. I felt it as I, Jacob – myself, but not myself – because it was vastly greater than myself. It took hold of me, struck fear into me at first. Yet as we wrestled I succumbed to the power – undefinable at first – which was being created – a force-field embracing both myself and the art piece, with which, as I strove and chipped away, I came into a relationship of understanding. I realised that this energy which I felt so intensely was the power of love. Yet it was a love beyond anything I had ever known – ineffable, yet demanding to be expressed. My greatest fear – the penetration of my body by that which I came to understand later as my Soul – was overwhelming – and this – some of this, you yourself felt as you re-created that two-dimensional image – that seemingly innocuous depiction. Some lines on paper, a few black scribbles and scratches, a wash of white, a mix of media, but energetically it was far more. It knocked you off your feet.

First version, E.E

We'd connected, you and I, like lovers in the physical act of creation, and you lost the power of your legs for a few days. Now, let me take you on further —

SYNCHRONICITY – Topping the Charts

When two people, two energies, come together, something which never existed before comes into being – a third is created. I was even trying to express this in my Rock Drill in a perverse way – bringing to birth a nightmare which didn't want – didn't ask to be born. This was creation by Rape. The dark aspect forcing into life the fruits of the outrage – a hideous seeding of a crop which is still being harvested in your time. How shall Man atone for his deeds committed in darkness? And what, you ask, has this to do with the Angel of Dark mien?

The voice I knew as Jacob Epstein had reasserted itself more distinctly as the message continued. Nevertheless I felt slightly nervous, unsure that I had grasped what he telling me.

Jacob, I don't understand you, even though what you say is correct in some detail. I was simply trying to make – well, not a copy – but my interpretation of your sculpture, pen and ink, paint and pencil. Two dimensional, as you say. Yet I was drawn in, and the deeper in I got, the more intensely involved, the more I began to feel these sensations. Hard to explain, but physical feelings – as though, instead of paint-brush or black pencil, it was a chisel I held in my hand, and I was carving directly through the paper, shaping something living and breathing under my hand. It was uncanny, yes. I was breaking into new ground. Not being taken over by you in the sense of possessed, but experiencing myself in a new and more intense way by merging with your energy.

Ah, yes, and this is what I feel when I make a portrait. I expand the sense of myself through diving into the energy of the other. So we have a kind of love-making in which the finished product is the offspring of the meeting. We are exploring the act of creation together.

ONCE MORE SYNCHRONICITY INTERVENES

During the time that I'd been typing out this chapter, copying out Jacob's words from the hand-written pages in my notebook, unbeknown to me, Crysse Morrison had been

DREAMING WORLDS AWAKE

visiting London. Whilst there she'd happened to drop in at the Epstein Memorial Exhibition which I'd mentioned at the beginning. One of his pieces in particular had impressed her – enough for her to pen a poem on the spot. A few days later she came to see me – we'd made this arrangement to have lunch together some weeks earlier.

Crysse is a writer, performance poet and playwright. She also leads writer's workshops all across Britain and Europe, and recently in the U.S. In addition to these activities, she also gives independent novel mentoring advice to many budding and established writers. It was Crysse who had reviewed and edited my, *Strange and Precious Thing* which had come out the previous year. Wearing her editorial hat, she'd been taking a look at this, my latest manuscript, a very brief glance, as she explained, to get some sense of what my new material was about. At this point, on this particular morning, I was roughly half way into what I'd envisioned as a short, 60 to 70 page book. We'd arranged this informal meeting as a preliminary to her giving it her fuller attention at some time in the future. It was at a rough draft stage and the ten or so pages featuring the three sculptures I'd chosen to write about had only just been typed. She hadn't seen them before and they lay open on the table between us. I wanted to tell her how I felt about the way they'd come into being; how unsure I had been when I began to feel that Jacob was actually speaking to me, and how Kuthumi had communicated his assurance that it was in fact so. But, as I saw her reach for the pages and begin reading, I hung back from putting all this into words. Better not say anything, I thought; it might set us off on another track, confuse the matter under discussion if I had to start explaining who this Kuthumi was.

I became aware as she turned one page and then another of a faint smile playing across her face. I sat, not wanting to interrupt her while she read, but could contain my curiosity no longer. 'Why the strange smile,' I asked. 'Something I've said?'

'I think this is going to sound like another of your synchronicities,' she grinned. 'I've just written a poem on this very piece of sculpture you're writing about here – began it on the train coming down to Bath.'

Second version, E.E.

Of course I wanted to see it :

DREAMING WORLDS AWAKE

JACOB MEETS THE ANGEL (after Epstein's statue)

I didn't know what to expect – would you?
An angel descending suddenly, heavily,
wings like tombstones, dishevelled hair,
staring eyes. More like gargoyle on acid,
than heavenly apparition.
He swung like a wrecking ball towards me,
clung to me, clouting my thigh.
I almost fell, and he held me,
his stony arms grasping, his huge legs
buckled under me. I should have felt pain,
but I didn't. I felt sustained.
It was what I had always wanted.
Maimed, and claimed.

Crysse Morrison, November 2009

Picking up the threads at the place where the pages had opened for us, Jacob was speaking to me about making a portrait, and working together, a co-creative act, and I'd just commented that I didn't quite understand the Dark Angel reference.

> *'You are working on it,' he'd said. You chose to explore it when your decided to make that drawing, because you'd already recognised what it represented for you. And that's why its energy kicked you so hard. Explore with me. You chose Black and White, a simple metaphor of duality we could say. Historically, since the Garden of Eden when Man and Woman tasted the forbidden fruit and looked for someone to blame, we have lived in this state, knowing Good and Evil, God and Devil, and all the other offspring of duality; right/wrong, order/chaos, pleasure/pain, love/hate, male/female, sensuality/ spirituality. Our first murder is committed, our first taste of shame. Adam and Eve are expelled from Paradise, and so it all begins. And how!*

OK, I'm with you so far. We've lived in this state ever since – managed to carry on until now, and only avoided blowing ourselves to smithereens by the skin of our teeth. But our luck could run out any second. Yeh?

SYNCHRONICITY – Topping the Charts

The prophecies give us 2012 as the make or break, and we're at the brink of this date. Then you had that dream, O Shaman. Black and White again – intensity of contrast. The core of the Earth disgorges that load of dark matter which She'd held onto since Man's awareness and his denial of awareness began. But with it come those primitive Earth-shifting Dragons intent on giving your comfort zone a good shake up.

Yes, I'm with you again.

I know. Some dream, and you dreamed it after all. But let's take it a step further. I don't have to spell out duality, but just for clarity — since the fall, as some religions call it – we, that's you and I, Humanity, we've become judgemental, learned to separate, right from wrong, compare self with not self and wage constant war against the Dark Other. Always attempting to eliminate what we cannot bear to look at and own in ourselves; the brutal, the savage, the ugly, the crippled. We first project it 'out there', and then try to annihilate it altogether. The Evil Empire, The Great Satan – always out there, somewhere else. Once, these two energies, Dark and Light co-existed. We called it Paradise, but it's a metaphor again for the Source, or Primal Unity from which we all came. Dark, Light; simply two energies. The two Divine energies of creation – meant to work together, supporting one another, loving one another. So why did they become separate? Choice. We chose to bite the apple.

The Divine Self chose to go on an exploration pathway because it saw that if it stood still and worked only with the energies which Creation had provided at the beginning, the whole universe would arrive at a state of stasis and finally crumble away. A New Energy had to be created, and that could only happen with the gift of Freedom. Or, put another way, to be new it must continually emerge out of the Unknown. And here we are! Creators of New Energy, sculpting and shaping a new reality into being.

And you wonder why your knees buckled at the Angel's touch. Your Divine Lover within touching distance.

OK, but I think you're going to have to clarify a bit more. If you don't mind. If this is a new reality, it doesn't exactly feel all that different. In fact rather the opposite. Worse, I'd say, if anything. Right now I'm feeling physically crippled and unsteady, not to mention dyspeptic and hung-over. How's that for divinely touched?

Early days.

Is that all? That's the best you can come up with? And another thing. What's so new about unconditional love? This is what we're talking about, isn't it? Present day psychology – at its best – works with this energy: Love; the power that heals. They shy from using the word; distance themselves from it by clothing it in clinically acceptable terms, positive regard and stuff, but...

Early days. We talk endlessly about love, analyse, sing about it, confuse it with romance, dismiss it as sentimentality, but it only becomes love when we experience it. We have to open up the place in here, behind these steel fenders.

Ribs. Heart.

Yes. Allow it in so that we begin to love ourselves – all the darkness in here, the self-loathing, self-doubt, the ugly self. All these disowned aspects acting as a drag anchor holding us back so we couldn't sail out into the unknown. The Old Self we decided – this divided self – brought into being as we developed intellectual knowledge – couldn't be trusted. We looked for rules to keep us in check and brought the commandments down from the mountain, the ten step program. Invented religion, then overthrew it and set up science in its place. We'd stared into the heavens looking for proof, but couldn't find any God out there, so declared Him dead. But God never was a Him – or a Her, beard or no beard. No Father Christmas, never was.

What is it? You're giving me your apprehensive look.

I don't know.

Maybe you don't want to hear what I'm about to say. Look at that image again, Jacob and the Angel, lovers in a tight embrace, wrestling into the night. The two of them, are they struggling, each intent on overcoming the other, or is something else going on? By morning it has become apparent that there is no winner. Never was mean to be, because they are one, belong to each other, once separate but now together, and in this, energetically, you are transformed. As you carve this energy with me, forming and shaping it, what happens? What happens in the cells of your body? What is being recognised by your DNA? Does it begin singing a new tune? Is that what's happening?

All right, I can feel a resistance building up. If you're uncomfortable we can take a break here, move on to something else.

Thankfully I'll agree to that, I certainly need to let it go a bit – give what you've said time to settle in. The shift from the level of consciousness I'm coming from and the one I may be stepping into feels too great to assimilate at one step.

OK then, let's bring in something different here. Tell me where you've been lately? Remember I've been watching you – chuckling to myself. Come! I think you've been doing a bit of earth shifting lately. Shall we look into this?

Earth shifting?

Yes, haven't you been visiting those old Dragons again? Let's see how things have moved on since you first encountered them in all their primitive power. What have they been up to, I wonder? Have they changed? They are real, you know – a Right Royal Pair, as John Moat said – a packet of energy rising up to meet you in a dream, and a right royal shake up of your comfortable cave. So, why not tell me all about it?

ZONE SHIFT

Revisiting the Dragons. Jacob's invitation to take a break and move on had been well meant, but as I contemplated the dream which I guessed he was referring to, I realised this wouldn't be any easier. I would need to step back into that level of consciousness if I was to pull the experience from what I could only call a 'far out place'. That was how the dream began, at least the fragments of it that had still been within my awareness as I woke. I'd held a lingering sense of having travelled beyond what the mind was capable of capturing; visited a locality beyond that of any dream state I had remembered visiting before.

If, as we are told, we often travel as we sleep, journeying to places and realms in our dream-bodies, etheric or astral bodies, which we never recall on entering our normal waking state, then in this dream I had travelled out, but also managed to bring back a taste of that far-away world. Yet I was struggling to find a way to express it. It didn't seem to 'sit' in my every-day head which wanted to 'make sense' of my experience. I was uncomfortable with something I was unable to fit into any of my boxes, and Jacob's welcome invitation to take a break from the earlier situation, felt like I was being asked to jump from the frying pan into the fire.

'This trip I made out into the unknown? Is this what you mean?' I asked. He nodded. I paused, drew a deep breath and began immersing myself into it, drawing it back, letting it wash over me until I was there with it again.

'Well, there's nothing much to it,' I said, sounding apologetic, feeling I ought to be reporting on some significant event. He seemed to smile. *'Just go on. Tell me what you see.'*

It's all vagueness, nothing extraordinary, nothing to get excited about. In fact if it's characterised by anything at all it's by its dullness. An empty landscape. Empty, like winter when everything's blotted out by snow, but this isn't even a white-out, it's a study in mid greys; clouds, smoke, ashes, drifting fog. And there I am, a stranger in a strange place, as if I've gone far out to a point beyond anything I can relate to. Certainly not some remote CGI box-office best-seller fantasy-planet with bizarre colours and surreal flora and fauna. This is a colourless land, featureless and insubstantial.

Disappointing? That it?

Well no, not quite, because I'm still watching, trying to make sense of it all, hoping for something to emerge. And after a while my patience is rewarded. I become aware of people, figures drifting by, but again nothing unusual, certainly no aliens or anything weird, in fact all too ordinary. But within me there's a growing feeling of my aloneness and my need to connect. I'm open to whatever comes along, happy to make friends, but these figures come and go – stream past, drifting like the smoke. I wait, and gradually I notice they're beginning to take on some slight individuality, becoming more distinct. Maybe this is because I'm signalling by the very fact of my patience that I am willing to enter into their world more fully.

A couple of men come up now, and I feel hopeful at last that we'll have something in common. So I go over making it obvious I'd like to talk. I try to engage them in conversation, but it's not really getting anywhere and they wander off. Maybe it's me, and they don't find me interesting. Then two more approach – tall, strong, intelligent eyes, good-looking, and if outward appearance is anything to go by they are just the kind of people I'd like to know better. We exchange a few words, but the conversation falls flat. I decide to make a bit more effort, but soon I realise they're more interested in each other, and it's not long before they pair off and drift away too. Maybe they're gay, but I'm fast losing confidence in myself. I don't seem to have what it takes, but I am disappointed now because I feel I am worth getting to know. So I turn my attention to a group of women. They're rather nondescript, but maybe they'll be easier to make friends with. On the surface they too seem dull; drab clothes, superficial conversation...

It's not your day, is it?

I told you this was going to be boring. How about we change the subject?

Huh! Just when it's about to get interesting? No, not now we've come this far. These women...

OK, if you must, but I'm not really enjoying this.

We're at the top of the hill now, and it lightens up and suddenly begins to feel familiar. I realise it's close to my old home where I lived with my parents until I left for London. My spirits lift, and excitedly I ask the women if they'd like to come with me to visit my old house. They respond warmly.

Now the whole scene begins to come alive. Having begun with the discomfort of dislocation, alone in an unrecognisable space, I'm now being brought back to earth. Memories awaken and flood back as I step into a recognisable world. The sun's warming my face; colours, scents and sounds are intensifying as we walk down the hill towards the house. But the women stop to point out something I haven't noticed. Apparently a lot of new building has recently gone up. I pause to take in the fact that a new housing estate is now covering the ground where suburban streets and parkland, gardens with their flowers and vegetables, sheds and workshops used to be. I'm horrified. Bulldozers are still at work turning over the land, uprooting trees and upturning children's swings. All the houses are alike; brand new, unoccupied, but characterless.

Everything here is uniform and soulless and without the individuality which the old dwellings had: a horrible sight/site in both senses of the word. An officially imposed New Estate built willy-nilly destroying the old way of life where people were good neighbours, skilled gardeners and craftspeople. And what has happened to the view? There used to be a beautiful vista opening out to the horizon, but it's gone, and left the people still living there resentful and hostile.

There is my old home at last, but it should be standing in its own spacious garden. It's now squeezed up along with the other old houses into a narrow, cramped terrace. In their relentless progress, the earth-shifting machines have created an avalanche of soil which is compressing everything, burying it and squashing it out of existence. I manage to peer through a slit in the doorway of the house I'd once lived in and I recognise the wallpaper. It's the one I knew had been there before we moved in, but my mother re-papered it with a much nicer pattern. The present occupant looks out at me. I wonder how she can bear to go on living there. Does she have to, I wonder? She throws me a suspicious glare. I'd felt so excited about finding this place again and showing it off to my new friends, but it's terrible to see what it has become.

I can sense my mother's presence behind me, and I compare her with this mean old woman who lives here now and realise how enlightened my mother, in her day, seems to me now in comparison, taking in anew how much she did in her life to create a good and nurturing home life. How spacious and light the interior had been, compared with now.
Well, this is it. This is where I wake up.

And it's not as if you don't know what was going on. Your dragons have become Earth-shifting machines. You knew all too well. You even conjured up a message from cyberspace the next day which confirmed all your own insights. You seem to need that confirmation – of what you already knew. And then you double checked, contacted Kuthumi and had him double confirm your knowledge. It would be nice to have him – his voice – here now.

UNIVERSAL FEEDBACK

If Kuthumi's comments are to make sense, I'll have to explain the state of mind I was in before the dream as it ties in with that message from the internet, a channelled message.

It was mid-winter when I'd contacted him, coming up to Christmas. I'd felt stuck, nothing happening, no inspiration, no dreams, feeling run down energy-wise. A sense that I wasn't moving and scolding myself for not doing enough. Yet when I tuned in to my own guidance sources, Higher Self, gnost, inner wisdom, or whatever you want to call them, all were telling me the same thing; "It may seem that nothing is happening, but a great deal is happening on levels you cannot see and don't yet sense."

Then along came the dream, this strange place where all was flat, drab and inconsequential for what seems like an interminably long time. I told Kuthumi about this state I was in, and he came back with this:—

Hibernating and gathering energy is often mistaken for being stuck. Sometimes it is just a gathering of energies, and I have to tell you that this time leading up to Christmas was this for many people who are open to such energies, and many of them were developing illnesses to justify the lack of energy and enthusiasm. I do not mean to belittle your experience by throwing it into a mass event... but so many of you use these times as an excuse to be hard on yourselves. You say you are procrastinating or avoiding, and lets be honest many of you do these things, but sometimes you just need a time out! This will be something for you to practice this year, tuning into when you need an energetic timeout!

I then went on to tell him about the dream from how it began, how it developed, witnessing the rampant destruction of my home as the Earth-moving machinery sweeps away all that has been, through to the place where I peered through the letterbox.

At some point just before I woke, I told him, I heard a voice, abusive, harsh, terrifying – yelling at me; **You're no**

good! You haven't done enough! Then this face sprang out at me, dark with bared teeth, and I told him how the shock hit me in the solar plexus as I realised for the first time just how potent this demon, my inner saboteur, was. As I woke back into consciousness, my body was gripped by what felt like a tight metallic corset, as if it was cellularly resisting having to recognise this savage aspect which had always been hidden inside.

It occurred to me later how much this sensation reflects your Rock Drill, the torso at least. But having the dream present it face-to-face and out in the open was very positive, I thought.

Then close on the heels of this dream an e-mail arrived. Whether, as you suggested, I conjured it myself from cyber-space is open to question, but my mouth opened with amazement as I read it. It seemed the universe was feeding back to me its affirmation of what was going on inside. When I showed it to Kuthumi he returned it with parts of it underlined.

An excerpt:—

"Although it may feel as though nothing much has been occurring of late, or perhaps there has been a great lull, <u>there has indeed been a great amount of restructuring and preparing occurring for our very next phase</u>.

The separation of the worlds occurred in September ... we broke off from the old reality and ventured into a very new one. This created enormous movement for the New Planet Earth, as she was pushed into a very new groove in the universe, now occupying a space within a very new and higher vibrating position.

During this time, anything and everything residing upon and within the earth was also pushed out of its old groove. An enormous amount of energy was required to create this movement, and many of us felt it with great intensity. <u>During this time, everything was pushed, so any dormant or remaining darkness within us was moved up and out as well</u> (just when we thought that most of our internal purging was over for awhile!). This was a massive undertaking and a monumental event.

Immediately preceding <u>this process that pushed us into a very new location</u>, many of us found ourselves in new homes, either through new changes with our current homes, or through literally moving to very new locations on the planet."

I have underlined a few points in the channelling, Kuthumi said, *that could be useful to read in isolation! Your dream was quite literal in the second half and you actually "analysed" it perfectly. In fact dreams right now are quite literal and extremely personal. For instance to dream of a childhood home for you is very different in meaning to how someone else would dream. It was very insightful to find your own translation.*

But I will give you some insight as to some other aspects of the dream which were in fact aspects of yourself.

I'd told Kuthumi that what I'd found disturbing in my dream was this sense of not being able to relate to people at a deep and meaningful level. Then the pain in seeing everything I'd known and loved, although not appreciated at the time in my youth, being obliterated by some nameless authority on high as they created this New Estate. I felt dis-located from this sanctioning authority, a mere bystander to all that was happening – not the author of it. I didn't seem to be coping at all well with this new location and needed to get back to my roots, only to discover them being swept away.

This sense that you cannot find connection with these people is a reflection of the sense you are not connecting with some very deep parts of yourself. And there are some parts that are not ready to communicate or connect consciously with you, but this is not a reflection of anything you are doing wrong or right. It is simply about the aspect and where you are right now. It is all perfect.

So if a part of you is not ready then that is fine. Keep an eye and ear out for the ones that are, and connect with them.

In the meantime you need to have an energetic lighthouse set up! By this I mean you are expanding out the energy that all parts of you are welcome and you are ready. And you are ready or else we would not be having these conversations and you most certainly would not have created that dream for yourself.

At this time you are bringing in lots of past aspects, from early life mostly. These will in turn bring others. Some you will be conscious of and others you will not. That does not matter. It is all really about being open to knowing there are these parts of yourself and they can integrate with ease and grace.

Yes there are times when you feel them physically and part of this is resistance, but that is easing for you. As you know you are indeed "cellularly sensitive" but thankfully now you know how to move through harder shifts with more ease than before.

Now to this "dark aspect" that is indeed your saboteur as you have known it before. Wow what a great insult to throw at you! And how proud I am for to recognise that to see and feel this is indeed a sign of "progress"!!

The physical sensation was almost a Pavlovian response, as anyone would react to this, and this is a sensation you have known many times even subconsciously. For a lot of people this would signal and mark the beginning of a huge slide into depression. This dark aspect can work so surreptitiously that in many it would trigger the response without the person even being conscious of its interaction. This is the hypnosis that so many people live within each day.

Those choosing the new energy though are blasting through this so that like you when this part of them comes up they see it is just a part of themselves and not something that controls them.

You will find it pops up again and the more you simply acknowledge this as just a part of you and not something to fear then it will "fall into line". It will not seem so 'big' and the physical reaction will also reduce.

When it does appear or makes some noise, of course the best thing to do is breathe.

The breath pulls you back to your centre. It clears and strengthens the connection to your essence and it is your essence that you want running the show and not just one or two aspects. It is your core which has clarity, that expresses without fear and without drama. It does not judge you and it most certainly knows you are doing all you can!

When your essence is asked to steer, then your aspects know you are truly ready for them.

* * *

Let us thank Kuthumi here for his welcome and very insightful input, and the lovely energy he shed and shared with us. We took a diversion, and diversions make for interesting journeys. Hopping onto a train, buying a ticket with a destination printed on it, and having a track, the rails already laid on which to travel – all that is one kind of journey. But setting out, not knowing where you're heading or what surprises are around the next bend – that's quite another kettle of fish.

I suppose all this has, on the surface of it, very little to do with making a portrait, but the work we're making together, this co-portrait of ours, is a journey into a sea of energy. Will it be rough or calm? Will it have depth and shallows, shifts of colour, shifts of temperature, icebergs, storms? I, the sculptor looking into you, and you the sculptor attempting to see into me. I can feel you getting uncomfortable again. I am staring into your depths and you don't like it. I sense a huge resistance brewing up. I think that old saboteur may be behind it. Things in there you don't want to own, but in this instance, counter to what you or others may suspect, they are not dark and shameful. We are shifting energy, because a whole New Estate is about to be built. And you are its architect.

OK, we took an interesting digression, you had your break, but that should make you all the more ready to resume our portrait project – our co-portraiting project.

You haven't changed much, have you? I feel like I'm caught sitting around outside the college door again, smoking, drinking coffee and planning to sneak off up Queensgate for another swim in the Serpentine. And you strolling in with your, 'Great day for woike.'

Yes, and isn't this fun, hey! So what were we talking about before we took time out? The Women, I think.

Well, yes, and we were still looking at your Angel Wrestling sculpture. We hadn't finished that, as I remember.

I took you away from that to discuss this – some new aspect which came to my mind. What came after my Jacob and the Angel? I was asking you that question, I think. Not directly after, not chronologically, but after you'd chosen to write about the three subjects which had interested you, Adam, Rock Drill and this Angel sculpture. Then I introduced the Risen Christ. Which was where we met, if you remember. Where I came into your life.

The *Christ in Majesty*? Was that what it was called? The the massive figure you were working on when I met you fifty years ago? He of The Big Feet?

A colossal Central being who'd passed through death's door, and presented Himself to the Women in the garden. They were the ones who had belief, didn't ask to see the wounds, like the man Thomas. They Knew – and were changed. My Kingdom is not of this World, he said, and at that time the world was not ready. The knowledge was taken on by the Marys, passed on down the centuries, carried through the stony places and the barren places where men failed to hear – because they were not ready. Men continued to build their structures, and take control, as they do when they're afraid.

Afraid?

Of Woman of Power, Spiritual Power.

And that brings me to my observation that you, also, were given the name Mary. And, I believe, you also had some interesting dreams a while ago concerning Mary. It was a dream which heralded another shift for you. This awakening into new consciousness – this new awareness which those who choose it are going through – happens in stages. And as Kuthumi told you recently, each shift is like climbing and reaching a high peak only to find there's yet another, even higher peak before you. But as you make each climb and the *going gets steeper, your skill and strength develops at each stage – which in turn takes you on and up to the next. And gradually it all gets easier and smoother.*

You integrate more and more aspects of yourself as you climb, and the Mary dreams were times when Mary, Mother of Christ, Mother of God was integrated. And this shift preceded your Shaman dream – which brings us to Integration of the Light/Dark aspect, and that brings us to all that you have experienced around the Jacob and the Angel work.

Remember you told me I'd been remiss not to take women seriously when I was making my portrait heads. "Where are the powerful women," you asked? Their time had not yet come, I said. And now I'm making amends, although I did portray the Annunciation in the midst of all the controversy and fuss over a few other pieces of my work. She was growing within me, in my consciousness, in her own time and in her own way.

You were young, and at a place where your time also had not yet come, and you were drawn to that young Mary figure I'd made some time before.

Yes, I loved it. Wished I could make something as powerful. The sculpture was powerful without being ... without shouting out loud. Feminine, youthful, and taking in, or trying to take in, all it meant to her to be the bearer of a divine force. The earthly vessel of Divine intervention.

'Fear not, Mary,' that Angel had said, when he came knocking one bright morning. A different angel, or one in another guise from the one who'd appeared to the biblical Jacob centuries before, yet posing another challenge to wrestle with. Who would believe her? How could she persuade Joseph, her betrothed, to take this on board? This teenager who he'd struggled to keep himself from so she could demonstrate to the satisfaction of all the neighbours in the district on their wedding day, that she'd been pure and intact. And here she is brazenly spinning him this tale of an angel at the door – and then, the obvious signs of her pregnancy. How was she to convince him? Yet she'd managed it somehow. What qualities did such a girl possess who could do that? And where, inside myself, did I find those qualities to bring her to

ZONE SHIFT

life? I am Epstein, the rapacious villain of the Rock Drill, the creator of that Oscar Wild memorial who outrages civilised society by endowing angels with genitals. Angel with genitals! How else would Gabriel, the Angel of Birth, accomplish his mission? Poke her with a lightning rod? Well, maybe that's what Joseph put to her when they argued. 'Is that what I'm expected to tell the neighbours?' he yells, bewildered, humiliated, angry. But, so the story goes, he also has a dream visitation, and falls into line.

Let's move on. Merging. One energy merging with another. Two coming together and creating a third. Something unique. A new being. Can we move once again towards the conundrum of the Dark Angel. Who it was that Jacob wrestled. His dark side. His hidden self. The self we all wish to conceal, or never to reveal or allow a voice to. Energies separated which once were unified. How are we to understand all this? This is man's conundrum. We wrestle with our darkest self, we're presented with our greatest fear at the same time as our Divinity. What a paradox. Yet what we meet is Love. Acceptance. I, the Darkness hold your hidden self, all that you reject. I can't tell you how it is: I can only invite you into yourself to experience complete acceptance. This is why we have met. This is why we sculpt together and transform energy. Big feet; big feat! Step into them and fly. No seat belt needed. What's the worst? You can only die. And you've done that already, many times. And so have I. But with you beside me we can build a new body – and that can be fun. Never attempted before. We have this thing called DNA to play with. We have a Field to play in. We have strings to carry our kites up into the blue. How about it? Come fly with me! And still have feet of Clay. What could be better?

IN A NUTSHELL

"Let us go then, you and I, when the evening is spread out against the sky, like a patient etherised upon a table... Let us go...."
T.S.Eliot, 'The Love Song of J. Alfred Prufrock'

I would never have chosen them for myself. I had a fair working knowledge of animal aspects already; Power animals, Totem animals, Pakauwah being just some of the names by which they're known. I'd worked with them previously but been out of contact for a decade or so before I felt the urge to invoke one again recently, so I wasn't at all surprised that they had changed in the meantime, for that is their nature. I knew already that these animal aspects shift because the way they appear to us evolves as our state of readiness expands. The shift reflects the level of our consciousness at the time.

When I'd called up power animals before, I was aware to some extent that I was throwing out a preference for the sort of animal I wanted. I can see now – perhaps I saw even then – that these preferences were coloured by a degree of ego, a need to find a non-human type of being I could identify with. In part I chose rather than allowing myself to invoke them with absolute trust in whatever decided to manifest. Nevertheless the images which arose in my mind then – lion with full and flowing mane, a black panther, a gentle deer, eagles, hawks, owls, honey bees as examples – all seemed to appear quite spontaneously, and I'm sure they held some very pertinent messages for me at the time. I'd soared on great outspread wings, up and over mountain tops, gaining a vantage point from where new perspectives opened up, new insights into life's issues. Yet when I felt the urge to reconnect with a totem animal again recently I anticipated that it was going to be different this time – perhaps a surprise.

After a lapse of several years I was more ready to trust the unknown. What I wasn't prepared for though was the fact that nothing appeared at all. I tried several times, emptying my mind, breathing deeply, letting go all expectation; yet still nothing came. Nothing except a repeated suggestion that I might find my animal in a book. I dismissed this as a random thought, but after quite some time and my patience growing thin, the suggestion persisted as though it was being whispered in my ear. So I decided I would act on it after all. Just open any old book? Perhaps. But it seemed reasonable to open one I knew had pages full of animals – and power animals at that. My inner voices didn't correct this reasoning, so I solemnly took down the book I had chosen and sat with it, breathing deeply and emptying my mind as before. But this time I 'knew' that when I opened it at random I would find my totem staring back at me.

"Now!" I heard, as clearly as if it had been spoken out loud. I opened it and the eyes which met my own were those of a hippopotamus!

I gulped. This was not what I'd expected. Never in my wildest dreams... But what was I saying? Here *was* 'the unexpected' large as life, and twice as incongruous, so why this immediate reaction to want to send her packing? Letting go expectation? Ready for the unknown? Who was I fooling? I smiled, and she smiled back. I roared with laughter: she roared back. My eyes then caught the headings to the text and I felt tingles down my back: MIDWIFE and REBIRTH.

HIPPOPOTAMUS in the lands of Ancient Egypt was the

midwife Goddess, Tawaret (Taueret, Taret). She not only presided over the mother's labour and the child's birth into human life, but accompanied it on its journey into a second life, initiating an awakened state of being born again. Of course this is a choice: no-one is forced to take the path of initiation. We come to it, or should come to it of our own free will. Anything other than a choice freely made will back-fire in one way or another, either on the one who persuaded us into it against our better judgement, or on ourselves, if we went against our better judgement. Yet even saying that is not to declare that such a mistake in any way condemns us, it only provides us with further learning. And all learning is fruitful, particularly when it leads to greater self-awareness and self-acceptance.

Tutunkhamen's tomb, I was intrigued to read, among all the jumble of other treasures, had contained three couches; The Hippopotamus Couch symbolising birth into physical form; The Cow Couch which corresponds to accessing the astral plane, and The Lion Couch which has to do with birthing the stellar body. What lesson then did Tawaret have for me? These three phases seemed to represent levels in spiritual consciousness with the hippopotamus earth-birthing phase coming first, but leading, if we so chose, to a rebirthing. What I'd felt personally over the last few months was a sense that a new physical birthing was in progress within me. Working with Jacob had taught me valuable lessons. It had brought about a deepening understanding of the energy that is Genius, the energy that expresses the God within us all. His carving of Jacob wrestling with the Angel vividly expresses his sense of life in the human body, his own instinctual energy, the erotic force, its passion for life and love passing into and merging with the powerful, intangible energy-body of the Spirit.

Since the moment Tawaret had looked out at me from that

page I had also been feeling the hippo very close to me and felt the reason she had chosen me was because my own body was undergoing a huge energy shift, and that was giving me a very hard time physically. I was glad to have her helping me to go through it, glad also to have the feeling of being in the flow of the great Nile with the marshes around it. I could see her clearly with her family rooting about in the shallows. I smelled with her the fertile mud where luscious papyrus and lotus grew, where tall reeds waved in the river-side breeze. But when I told Kuthumi about my encounter with Tawaret, my new Totem Animal, I was in for another surprise.

What a powerful totem and such an amazing way to find your connection with her. Yes this totem has many ties to your past lives in Egypt (which we will get to) but first I want you to truly connect with the energy of hippo in general. Acknowledge what a powerful animal this is. They appear cumbersome and "fat" but they are in fact incredibly powerful animals. Despite their size they are fast, and even though they do not have fangs, claws or poison they are one of the most deadly animals in Africa. So yes this is a wonderful reflection for you to understand that our physicality is not a limit to our expression. That despite how we look or feel, we all have innate qualities that make us as powerful as anyone else.

To see your hippo in the waters of the Nile is all about nurturing, yes just as you felt it. Because this is also how you knew the hippos in your time in Egypt. So now let us talk about your time in Egypt:-

This life was around 2000 BC, so the pyramids were around 500 years old, but you had not seen them as you lived in a village quite south on the Nile, past modern-day Thebes but ahead of the Aswan region. You were a midwife and so you were very connected with Tawaret, the hippo goddess who came in to protect and support not just the mother and child but also you. For in your time midwives were a very sacred role and part of society. You were crucial for the safety of childbirth, ensuring heirs and successors were born healthy and safe. Your role was not just about delivering children, it was about maintaining society. Because if children were not born safely then how would society develop or continue?

You saw something more to all this though. You saw the joy and magic in being part of a new beginning. You knew people were so invested in the afterlife, as your Pharaohs built their tombs and people spent their savings on their preservation. It upset you that the same grandeur was not lavished on a birth. After all this was the beginning of the beautiful cycle that ended in the afterworld. Yes royalty celebrated their births in immense ways but this was political. Your job was simply done when the child was breathing and the mother's bleeding (if any) stopped.

This made you sad some days but you found ways to celebrate in your own way. As you prepared for each birth you would go to temple, burn incense and pray to Tawaret, And you would do so after each birth also. There were times when the birth was not so successful and you would question Tawaret and ask her why that birth had been abandoned by her. You never got an answer though.

One day you sat upon the banks of the Nile and you saw a small family of hippos in the water. You looked and saw that one female had a baby with her and you smiled. "Ah Tawaret, you have birthed your own child," you called out to her and she turned to look at you. Nearby another female grazed and you wondered why she had no baby when it was clearly the season and she was of age. As you looked closer you could see that she had some remnants of afterbirth hanging below her tail and you realised that she had just given birth. But there was no baby nearby.

"It must have died," you realised and that sadness you knew when such things happened came upon you.

"Even your symbol must suffer such things," you called to Tawaret and this time you heard a reply.

"It is the way of things for all beings," you heard and you nodded.

"Yes it is just the way of things," you replied.

This did not heal completely your sadness when another baby was lost but you knew in your heart now that it was simply the way of things.

IN A NUTSHELL

So your totem has many layers to her. Research her more if you feel you would gain more insights, because each time she will lead you to more connections and insights!

* * *

Some time later – it had been that long, dreary winter; the cold, months of freezing temperatures alternating with melting snows which found their way into the house through cracks the ice had scored with her claws, then heavy rain driven by northerly gales – I was thinking I hadn't seen Tawaret for a while. She was there as I'd succumbed to a dose of flu in mid-March, ironically just as winter seemed to be loosening its grip at last. She'd given me some healing which shortened the worst period of the viral infection, but since then I'd only been aware of a pair of eyes looking at me. They could have belonged to any animal. Totem animals change their appearance, of that I was aware, and I'd vaguely wondered if a new one was in the offing. But it wasn't until I caught the transcript of a current talk by Adamus Saint-Germain, who, with the kind of synchronicity I'm beginning to take for granted, brought the subject of our Pakuawah up, that I thought I'd see if Tawaret had indeed changed.

Once more I breathed deeply and slowly, sat with quiet mind and open heart, attuned to my Higher Self, but when the word Cow came up my immediate reaction was once again to dismiss it. My mind playing a joke. 'You just cannot be serious,' as some old tennis player once said! I breathed and sat, and tuned in again. 'Cow,' repeated my inner voice. I sat in puzzled silence quite some while. Cow? Whatever kind of *Power* animal is that? How long I sat there in bemused refusal I don't know, but suddenly the lightbulb lit up. Tutunkhamen's tomb! The Cow Couch! But what did it mean for me? Why had she chosen me – or why had I chosen her? I know the cow is sacred to the Hindus, and is a nurturing mother figure, but I don't feel at all Cowy.

DREAMING WORLDS AWAKE

Expect the unexpected when it comes to totems! Kuthumi had said. *And no they don't always appear in forms that are well regarded by you. I will give you another aspect to a cow though– they are very symbolic of English countryside, if that means anything to you as well.*
Remember that totems can also be just pockets of energy and not really have a recognisable form! It is more fruitful to just feel what they are carrying for you and remember they serve you. So when you call upon one you direct it!
Tawaret is still around though...she just wants to play in a new way.

"EXPECT THE UNEXPECTED"

There's such a tingle of excitement in that phrase. How will the unexpected manifest? Asking that very question presupposes that our mind, that thinking process we default to so often, so readily, will come up with an answer. By now though I should have learned to set aside the default reaction which looks for answers: The Unexpected finds its own ways of manifesting. Yet how ready I am still to dismiss it when it does. Even now I catch myself wondering, What next? And if it manifests how will I react? React rather than accept or respond. Can I handle the Red Hot Now when it ups and bites me, or shall I struggle in confusion and frustration, not knowing what to make of it?

I dream. In this new dream I am some kind of post box – very new tech, made of metal with several glass windows, so it feels extremely constricting, not only due to the materials it is made from but by the fact that I am having to program it in order to do a simple task. I'm required, or so it seems, to address an item ready for posting. As tasks go this shouldn't be the trickiest bit of rocket science I'd ever been faced with. Normally, in the time-honoured way, all I'd have to do would be to take a paper envelope and write an address on it. But this glass and metal system requires me to enter different parts of the address in separate windows. It's such a complex

IN A NUTSHELL

operation it must have been devised by some techno-wiz male-brain person, and I've got myself into it in some way I can't remember. I wake with my whole body tightly seized up.

Struggling to understand, still viewing the dream image logically, I conclude that I'm trapped inside this metal and glass box contraption which, compared to the Old handwritten envelope technology, represents the New. This dream is turning into the worst kind of nightmare. Imprisoned by New Energy!

> *Yes wasn't it perfect*, said Kuthumi. *Because sometimes it seems surrendering to the new energy is more complicated....and that you have just given yourself a new set of guidelines to constrict you.*
>
> *This part of you that keeps resisting the new – your H.S. keeps giving you the insights and this is all well, but this is just continuing the dance. Its time to actually talk with the aspect. It's a past-life one, so let us tell the story now:–*

However, before I got to read the story which Kuthumi was about to disclose, I had another, and possibly the most significant dream I've ever had. But first, set out below, is the past-life story followed by the dream I was having simultaneously.

> *Understandably we now go back to Ancient Egypt to a temple where you were a priestess. It was upon the banks of the Nile and indeed this temple was dedicated to Tawaret and Nut. It was an odd combination but it worked. As they are both symbols of the feminine, your temple became a place for women to worship and many with fertility problems or wanting a daughter to find marriage came there to worship. It was a place that exuded softness and gentility so much that the queens and princesses would come there as a sort of retreat.*
>
> *But as with all religions (and this ties to your first [Tawaret] dream) there were political elements. Now you were not near Karnak but close enough that any reforms had to be enacted within your temple.*

DREAMING WORLDS AWAKE

There came the day that your priestesses were told that you could no longer perform fertility ceremonies for royalty, this was the duty and privilege of those at Karnak! But one day a princess arrived to you upon horseback, she had disguised herself to escape the palace and she was crying.

She had been married two years and had not fallen pregnant. She was the talk of the palace and her husband had begun to speak of divorce. The priestesses and priests of Karnak had been performing ceremony for her but with no results. You were her last hope and under the pact of secrecy you performed the ceremony and sent her on her way home.

Unfortunately someone did see her make her way to your temple and the Pharaoh dragged the truth from her. But it was not the Pharaoh who ordered the high priest to come to you, they did this of their own accord upon hearing what had happened.

They dragged you before the other priestesses and beat you to within an inch of your death. The five of them stood over your limp, battered body and the eldest shouted, "Let this be a lesson to the rest of you. Remember your place. Remember who is important!"

It was a miracle you survived but you did and even in this you showed all that you must be adored by the gods. You never walked properly again though, and the pains in your body were continuous, but each day you would rise above this because in your heart you knew you had done no wrong.

One day about nine months later you stood upon the portico of the temple and looked up to the sky, thanking Ra for his beauty. Another priestess came up beside you –

"There has been news from the palace. The princess has birthed a son."

As tears fell down your face the pain in your legs seemed to disappear for a moment.

"It was worth it," you whispered

"Truly! You can truly say this after escaping death at the hands of those pigs?" The other priestess was aghast.

"I did what I knew was right and in the end I achieved what I promised I would. There is nothing more to life than that. These pains are mere testimony and side effects of this," you said.

The priestess shook her head and walked away.

IN A NUTSHELL

> *This is the aspect that wants to come home now. She wants to see how being your truth can be a life without being punished. She wants to see how trying new things, or breaking rules doesn't mean you will get beaten, but celebrated! When these anxieties come up, remind them that all is safe. There is no hierarchy to answer to anymore. Its just you! And all is well and worth it.*

Yet before I'd had chance to read this message from Kuthumi – it was still travelling towards me on an email from Australia, the other side of the world – I was having the following dream:–

I am standing in a room…. It feels like it's in a temple…. I'm looking down on a table covered with a white sheet. Upon it, lying before me with her head to my left, is the most remarkable body of a female, and it's this head I take in most clearly. She's wearing a crown, but not the circlet sort of crown we're used to. It is more like an extension of the head, an elongated oval coming to a slight point at the top. The whole figure is composed of billions of tiny – I wouldn't say diamonds because, although they are brilliantly shimmering, flashing with colour, they seem much softer, subtler than diamonds. I'm gazing at a substance which is like a myriad crystalline stars, but not covering just the surface. The whole body is transparent, and looking into it I feel I'm being drawn deeper and deeper into an infinite astral complex.

As my eyes travel down from the face to the neck and shoulders I notice that the right shoulder and arm lying nearest to me is more developed than the other. Then looking further down I see that the body as a whole is not yet complete. The legs, for instance are not quite all there. It is a 'work in progress' or in process of being created. The room reminds me of an operating theatre, or a 'theatre of operation' as well as being part of a temple. For some time, regarding this wonderful body, I am awestruck. She is indeed a Goddess, and it seems certain that she is Nut. But as I watch I am growingly conscious of the nature of the process I am observing. I become aware that opposite me, the other side of the table, stands an invisible male figure, but I'm certain he is there, hidden, possibly behind the wall, pillar or a curtain. It is this figure who is the actual creator of the body on the table. As I watch now, I begin to feel very uncomfortable.

Something in me rebels. The operation in progress, rather like a medical procedure, begins to feel distasteful to me. I begin to see that this wonderful female body is having this done *to* her. The male figure, the creator, (or figures, because I sense that there are male assistants with him), is performing an operation to create a 'mother' whose role is to be constantly available as a producer of milk, and although she objects to this role and protects her breasts from being exploited, the creator figure is getting around her attempts at defence by adding a third breast to her body so that the milk will be 'on tap' for anyone who comes to her. Not only that, but these men are planning to implant a very tiny baby in her chest, (an embryo?) as this will ensure that the milk supply will go on and on. I am appalled at what I am witnessing, but as my angry feelings mount, a new figure comes onto the scene.

Through a doorway at my right steps a stunningly beautiful priestess. She stands at the foot of the table and I know immediately that she is Priestess of Nut. Her whole bearing is magnificently poised and confident. She moves with grace and suppleness, and has the demeanour of one who has the whole situation in hand. She radiates common sense and compassion, but will also stand no nonsense. She is not dressed in ancient Egyptian robes, she is a young woman of today. Her robe is a deep red, thick silk or satin which clings to her strong and healthy body, enhancing its beauty, revealing her contours without being overtly sexy. I immediately relax in her presence knowing I can leave it all to her.

Here I wake up. (Deep red is not a colour I'd associate with a priestess. However...)

The first thing that struck my about this dream was my extremely angry reaction as I observed the 'operation'. The male figure, who I saw as The Creator, was acting completely unethically by imposing his agenda on the Goddess, who, lying face up and unconscious on the table, was in his power. I get very angry when cows themselves are subjected to scientific procedures which make them give far too much milk for their own good. As observer in the dream, I'd felt a sense that this Goddess was being disempowered by the masculine God figure. As I thought it over later I noticed this ambiguity, knowing that I see this 'Goddess' as perhaps an energetic metaphor for 'The Great Mother' archetype, something divine and miraculous who has infinite power to nurture and heal all who come to her, yet at the same time she's related to the human feminine aspect of 'mother'.

I feel this dream has pointed to some awkward questions; is there an unconscious aspect to Divinity? And perhaps; is there a dark side to Divinity as seen in the form of a male God? In the dream the Goddess was asleep and the Creator was hidden. Psychologically that which appears hidden is unconsciously present, but without our being aware of it, it is nevertheless very much alive because we project it onto the outer world. Our image of 'God' at any one time, according to our state of consciousness, is a man-made (and very distorted and unbalanced) projection.

Thinking this over, discussing it with Michael, one thing the dream appeared to demonstrate was how we tend to place the male thinking function (personified by the medical scientist 'creator' here) above all other qualities and set it up over other aspects of intelligence. In other words, we deify it. It illustrated one of the 'classic' psychological theories about projection and how men often treat wives or partners like mothers when they project their unconscious agendas on the Other. Our cultural programming produces an adult man who has learned to suppress or deny his feminine and his infant aspects. He plays up to the role of masculinity expected of him. As head of the household he must appear to be God-like in the eyes of wife and children, yet unconsciously, like the infant, he looks for a partner who will 'nourish' him, love him however badly he behaves, and supply all his physical needs. Also like the infant he will use ploys which play on her unconscious programming which wants to respond to those needs. If, as in some cultures still today, he manages to confine her to her biological/instinctual role, denies her access to the mind, to education, he can keep her always 'on tap'.

Yet the dream was also showing me that the priestess function came to the fore here. We talked about the colour she was dressed in. Red, I said, is for me, the life-force, fire, blood, passion, poppies, roses, rubies, garnets. She serves and mediates the Goddess presence to us. Yet ... the Goddess herself ? Subject to the male agenda? What's going on here?

What a rich dream in every sense. You have managed to explore the duality of divinity in a very rich sense and all your philosophising upon it is "correct".

I am going to go into the more personal aspects for you though, as there is nothing to add to yours or Michael's insights. The real key to seeing what you show yourself in dreams is to connect with the truly personal significance of the images and sensations. This is not to trivialise your other insights but I just want to take you in deeper.

Whenever you see a human form in a dream it is representative of an aspect of yourself. Nut here is your divine feminine as you see her. She is brilliant, ethereal, slightly unbalanced and being worked on! Yes the male figure is working on her and this is your masculine. You keep it in the background, almost denying its existence and yet you are aware of it. This fear that it can control or shape your feminine is deserved. But you show yourself that you have nothing to worry about for the human goddess in you steps in as the protector.

Yes she is strong, and though you see her as a priestess and not a goddess you know she is just as powerful. The real beauty is that the three can now work together in balance.

The red is very significant as it does mean all the things you say...it is also the vibration of your spirit family, and having her dressed as such is her way to let you know that while she is "human" she has not forgotten her heritage. Within her is the balance of the invisible male and the ethereal expanding female – overseeing them both to balance them is the priestess.

DREAMING WORLDS AWAKE

You may not be done with Nut just yet...but your visits now can be very gentle and nurturing.

Michael added as an afterthought, and I wish I'd thought of it myself, 'What we have here is the Walnut: the left brain/right brain; masculine/feminine mind within one shell. When they work together there is, in a nutshell, the balanced and complete human being.'

"Let us go then, you and I, when the evening is spread out against the sky ..."

... but the lady's now awake, and more than ready to partake.

TALE OF A FISH

One last story.

I come upon a stream among rocks and trees winding cool clear cold and deep, dark in places, inviting, I step up to the edge, senses awake, sandy-soft pebble-hard under foot, in my nostrils fresh silver-green in a rush of swirling air and water and interlaced branches sway of fronds smell of fern moss and frog-leap leppings, I shiver, not knowing but feeling, feeling tall like reeds wind-blown, bent forward, looking.

Here I stand at the water's edge, and growing in me is the sense that I'm here for some purpose. People around are playing, laughing behind me, having fun on the grass, but I'm drawn to the water, and seem to be holding something in my hand, a glass container. Jam jar, perhaps. Yes, it's a fish in a jar, and I've come here so I can let it go into the stream to be invigorated and cleaned by the swift running water. I'm allowing it this new sensation of swimming freely without bounds. I've owned this fish, it's been at home with me all its life, kept safe, cared for lovingly in a glass tank where I've tended it, fed it, changed its water. But now today I'm going to let it go, for however careful you are about welfare, life behind glass walls has its problems. Disease can occur, bought fish-food can never be as good as the real thing. So a few minutes in this flow of natural living water will do it the world of good.

I tilt the jar and as the water pours out it carries the fish into the flow of the stream. I'm watching carefully, not letting her out of my sight because I need to recapture her to take her back home when I judge she's had enough. So I follow, step down into the water too, the better to keep my eye on her.

DREAMING WORLDS AWAKE

The swell against my legs surprises by its power and the quality of lucidity it bestows. The fish swims round my feet at first, delighted at finding herself part of this rippling expanse for the first time in her life. And I'm thrilled, as her instinct seems to tell her everything she needs to know about the element she's in. She circles around, exploring, darting under the ochre rooty, bank-side clay, into some crow's foot shadowy weeds, her body twisting, tail flicking, widening her exploration. She dives till I lose sight of her and then, surfacing again, I catch sight of a quicksilver body heading a trail of bubbles like a comet.

But I grow anxious as I watch her swim further and further up stream, disappearing into dark depths. Yet arcing this way and that against the power of the current, she's clearly displaying her strength and courage.

My body, by contrast, tenses as I imagine all the possible dangers; traps and sharp snags, predators, mill-races, weirs, whirlpools. But she negotiates the current intelligently, brilliantly, leaping rills and falls, streaking away into the distance, until I realise that I can let her go, release her unconditionally into the flow of her natural element.

Dive into your creativity. Dive even deeper. Like the fish being released into unknown waters – keep moving because you know your surrounds intimately even though you have not been in them before. It's just like what you know ... there are just more resources and more to explore. The gates are open and you are stepping through. Namaste.

CODA

LION STORY, or CODA

Coda: A Tail; a short passage added at the end of a composition to round it off.

Drawn to the sun after a long and miserable winter and a disappointing spring, I'm having a short, and, why not say it? a well-deserved break in my favourite Mediterranean city.

The coffee here's always good. You can rely on it, and somehow even though I try to buy the same blend back home in England, it never tastes so wonderful as it does on a morning like this, sipping a cup at a pavement café, lazily watching people walking to and fro' on their way to work, to shop, to meet friends. There's a purposefulness in the way they go about their business, but it's without the hurry, minus the lines of stress we see so often on the faces of people back home. This is what it's all about; an opportunity to let go some of my own unnecessary tensions. Soon though I notice the general pace of the passers-by picking up. There's a sudden sense of excitement – a buzz – people talking to one another. Stirred by curiosity, I pay for my coffee and join what is now becoming a small crowd heading in one direction.

We seem to be moving towards the main square, and all the while the excitement is growing. Once in the piazza the crowd begins to turn its attention to the street on the far side which also leads into the square. It too is thronged with people moving towards the square. It's beginning to look more like a procession. People around me are in a state of anticipation, murmuring and pointing as if they know what it's all about. This is why they have gathered. As the procession draws nearer I notice that it's led by two women, one middle aged, the other older. Although their clothing doesn't differentiate them all that much from the rest, you can tell they are not of the crowd; they both have an air of authority; a commanding, but calm and confident presence, with a somewhat regal bearing. Who can they be?

The word now in the square is that these two women are bringing with them a fierce beast, but at first I can't see for all the jostling heads and shoulders, what kind of animal it is. I wonder if there is to be an event, something like when wild bulls are let loose and young men test themselves for bravery and agility by chasing them through narrow streets and round the main piazza. As the procession headed by the two women draws nearer I slowly begin to take in that this animal is a lion and that it's walking between them. I glimpse it for a moment, but it's not on all fours, it's standing upright on its hind legs, rather like a human. As the realisation dawns that it is a lion, I grasp the fact that the narrow street is funnelling the whole procession directly towards me.

The group are coming closer and closer, and suddenly I began to panic. I am right in the path of the lion. I am overcome with, what I can only describe as, *actual mortal terror*, and looking for escape I see a doorway to my left. I grab the handle, open the door and charge into a dark corridor. Once inside I feel safe: safe in the darkness. But for how long?

Desperate for greater safety, I run further and further down this dark corridor until I see that there are other doors opening off. I open one, but as I start to rush through it, light from the street outside streams in, and I realise that I wasn't safe at all; the lion could come in through any of these doors at any time.

I sit up staring into total darkness with my heart beating in terror.

* * *

CODA

I sat up in bed in the dark for a long time, knowing that this had been a dream, but my heart was thumping so fast that that in itself was alarming. Gradually, as I sat there trying to calm myself, I began puzzling about the dream, trying to understand it, but also surprised to have found myself with a degree of fear which I never expected to have experience in my life again.

DREAMING WORLDS AWAKE

Next day I began writing details down to get it clearer. I took in the fact that I had turned to the dark corridor in order to find safety. Gone back into *the darkness of unconsciousness, into my dark side,* rather than stay outside in the full light of day. I struggled to understand where this intense fear had come from.

As I was writing these thoughts down there was a voice somewhere in the background telling me to look at the possibility that the Lion might be the third totem or power animal; the third of the couches in Tutunkhamen's tomb. (The Hippopotamus, The Cow, and The Lion.) I kept dismissing this voice as it was interfering with my thoughts as I wrote, yet it came again and again until I decided I'd better take it more seriously and look into it. As I did, things began to fall into place. I suddenly saw the two female figures as Tawaret and Nut, or the two priestesses who between them were bringing the male Lion down the street and into the public arena in broad daylight. I knew that in the dream they had been perfectly 'in control', that is to say, walking fearlessly and confidently, knowing that the crowd were waiting for them to present the Lion to them. I began to see the Lion as King of the Beasts, magnificent in his own right, and although wild, fearsome and deadly, the crowd were waiting in anticipation of the honour this presentation bestowed on them. Only *I* was the one overtaken by fear, the one who retreated into the supposed safety of the darkness which turned out not to be safe after all.

Beautiful, said Kuthumi. We get so good at running and hiding from parts of ourselves – but they will always find us. And there is no guarantee they will eat us!

Yes the women represented these priestesses... but also remember that they were no different from the rest of the crowd – it was how they carried themselves that let you know this. They knew they were no different either – but they knew themselves

CODA

and they knew they could walk with the "lion" That was what set them apart!

Now, what am I to make of this? The priestesses of Tawaret and Nut, representing animal aspects of the divine feminine, carry themselves with confidence and know themselves as co-equals with the Lion. Could the Lion who terrified me be the divine masculine, or an aspect of the Male Creator who was present in my Nut dream? Either way, he is an aspect of me, yet I see him in a way which terrifies me. As a deadly powerful male, does he represent the killer in me? Ruthless in pursuit of his prey? I head into my dark side, the shadow, the state of unawareness, thinking I shall be safe from him there.

The lion for you is whatever part of your power that you fear! Yes it is masculine, it is a hunter, it is ruthless, it devours. And these are all aspects of you that you fear will take over if you step into your power.

It is now time to trust that stepping into your grandeur will not let these parts of you go into imbalance (you don't need to escort your power with female guards!) That the lion walked on hind legs shows he had been "humanised", that the power was transformed.

Trust that you can balance these parts of you that fear the "dark" parts taking over. You can "transform" them to walk with you in balance.

Namaste, Kuthumi.

DREAMING WORLDS AWAKE

THE JOURNEY I TOOK

The journey I took, the playground I found,
Brought me friends to delight and amaze me.
The merry-go-round spun me round and around,
And I danced to the music it played me.

But the tempo slowed down, my feet met the ground,
And the dance then took several new turns.
The journey went sideways, up, inwards and down,
As it twirled me and spiraled and whirled.

Then I knew that I wanted to be on my own
Just to see how it went, how it goes
When a calm has descended and day's light is ended,
But I found that I'm never alone.

I can take solo flight, pas de deux through the night,
Paso doble with Sun or with Moon,
Drink deep of the wine, ask the crowd home to dine,
Sup singly or share cup and spoon.

So when all's said and done, dear, and all hearts are one,
Let's reach out our hands, dear, and welcome the Sun.
For the world will spin on, dear, but shining anew,
With hatred all gone, dear, and fighting ceased too,
We'll tango together, an' I'll celebrate You.

I AM THE CREATOR ALSO

"All is well in all of creation, therefore let's have a celebration!"
Adamus — Saint-Germain, January 2011.

ACKNOWLEDGEMENTS

I would like to express my gratitude for all the support and encouragement I have received throughout the writing of this miscellany, but firstly I must mention contributors who have allowed their individual 'voices' to be presented under the heading of Correspondence. In particular, John Moat who gave his blessings to the inclusion of a letter he wrote to me; Crysse Morrison for her poem, 'Jacob Meets the Angel', written after her visit to the Epstein 50th memorial exhibition in London; Marisa Calvi for her personal contribution, but also for acting as channeller for the invaluable input of the Ascended Master Kuthumi, and of course Kuthumi himself for allowing portions of our dialogue over the last two years to be included. Also, to the renowned sculptor Sir Jacob Epstein, a special thank you. Crysse Morrison, instrumental in the past for helping to bring my last novel to fruition with her wise and insightful editing, was sadly, due to pressure of work, unable to give the same attention to this new book. Nevertheless she managed to overlight and support its unfolding with her creative spirit. My thanks also to Robert Palmer for his invaluable proof-reading and typesetting skills, conducting us through the process the while on diverse literary, narrative and amusing excursions. My thanks, last but not least, to Michael my husband for his helpful reading, his patience and quiet encouragement.

www.ingramcontent.com/pod-product-compliance
Lightning Source LLC
Chambersburg PA
CBHW031404040426
42444CB00005B/408